CHILDREN
OF THE
PAPER CRANE

Sadako Sasaki is pictured here, front row center, with the relay team of sixth-graders from the Bamboo Class—a few months before she developed the "A-bomb disease."

CHILDREN OF THE PAPER CRANE

The Story of Sadako Sasaki and
Her Struggle with the A-Bomb Disease

Masamoto Nasu

Translated by Elizabeth W. Baldwin,
Steven L. Leeper, and Kyoko Yoshida

NORTH CASTLE BOOKS

Armonk, New York
London, England

First trade edition, 1996

Library of Congress Cataloging-in-Publication Data

Nasu, Masamoto, 1942–
[Orizuru no kodomotachi. English]
Children of the paper crane : the story of Sadako Sasaki and her struggle
with the A-bomb disease / Masamoto Nasu : translated by Elizabeth W. Baldwin,
Steven L. Leeper, and Kyoko Yoshida.
p.   cm.
"A North castle book."
Previously published: 1991.
ISBN 1-56324-801-8 (alk. paper)
1. Sasaki, Sadako, 1943–1955.
2. Leukemia in children—Pateients—Japan—Hiroshima-shi—Biography.
3. Atomic bomb.
4. Hiroshima-shi (Japan)—History—Bombardment, 1945.
I. Title.
RJ416.L4S27613   1996
362.1′98929419′0092—dc20
[B]
96-2047
CIP
Printed in the United States of America

The paper used in this publication meets the minimum requirements of
American National Standard for Information Sciences—
Permanence of Paper for Printed Library Materials,
ANSI Z 39.48-1984.

♾

MV (p)   10   9   8   7   6   5   4   3   2   1

North Castle Books
An imprint of M. E. Sharpe, Inc.

Contents

Translators' Preface / vii

Part I

1
Field Day / 3

2
The Time of Her Life / 17

3
Remnants of Evil / 39

4
Presentiment of Death / 61

5
A Crane That Can't Fly / 79

Part II

6
Those Left Behind / 109

7
Overcoming the Grief / 135

8
A Cry for Peace / 153

9
Rest in Peace, My Friend / 179

10
A Genealogy of Paper Cranes / 197

Author's Note / 213

About the Author / 217

About the Translators / 219

How to Fold a Paper Crane / 220

Translators' Preface

This translation is the first detailed English version of the story of Sadako Sasaki. Sadako experienced the atomic bombing of Hiroshima when she was two years old. Masamoto Nasu was three. Sadako died at the age of twelve and became the inspiration for a monument to memorialize the many children struck down by the bomb. Nasu became a best-selling author of humorous children's books. This account of Sadako's death and the movement to build a memorial statue is nothing like his other works. What made him write it?

Although Sadako and Nasu grew up in a city gripped by harrowing memories, the reality of that cataclysm was elusive to those who had survived it as small children. Nasu has said he wanted to know more about the massive tragedy towering in his past and to create a record in his own voice for his own children. But his curiosity went beyond the bombing itself.

Though several other books about Sadako have been published in Japanese, they focus on what Nasu calls the "beautified tragedy" of her death. Nasu is the only author to deal seriously with the statue movement. He had donated to the movement when he was in junior high school and then found himself attending high school with Nobuhiko Jigo and other members of Sadako's class. He discovered that Nobuhiko and the others were strangely reluctant to discuss that part of their past. Why were they so reticent about a project that had dominated their junior high years and brought them a measure of fame? The author's curiosity about the movement became a part of his motivation to tell an important story in his city's past.

Fortunately, Sadako's family and the other key figures talked to him freely. Because they believed Nasu should try to communicate their point of view accurately, even Sadako's classmates broke their silence for him. For two years Nasu researched the girl, the movement, and the times in order to set the story down before time could erode the memories further.

Like thousands of other survivors of Hiroshima and Nagasaki, Sadako was struck down by radiation-induced disease at a time when the bombings themselves were already history. Always energetic, this young girl refused to abandon her enthusiasm for life just because she happened to be sick. As she lay in her hospital bed, Sadako remained cheerful and kind, and, of course, she folded her paper cranes. She was also careful not to give others pain by letting them know she knew she was dying. But there were others who also died beautifully and courageously. What made Sadako Sasaki the inspiration for a monument that attracted attention around the world?

A coincidence of people, events, and timing combined to place Sadako at the center of a movement. Her teacher, Tsuyoshi Nomura, molded his class into a tight group that valued looking after its own. Sadako's death left them with an intense sense of emptiness, a need to express something to her. At just the right time, that group was discovered by Ichiro Kawamoto, a young man with a burning mission. Kawamoto felt it was time for Hiroshima to remember the children she had lost—and he was not the sort to wait for more powerful people to see the need. Sadako's classmates, so strongly bonded to one another, were the ideal group for him to encourage and guide.

But Kawamoto and Sadako's classmates, however strongly

motivated, could not have germinated a major movement without a hospitable national climate. The American military, while occupying Japan from 1945 to 1952, was busy overseeing the restructuring of Japan's new political and social order. Voices raised in criticism of American acts—particularly the dropping of the atomic bomb—were considered a threat. A Press Code Order from General Headquarters in 1945 forbade the Japanese to print or broadcast anything relating to the atomic bombings. Apparently those bombs, having massively slaughtered man and woman, young and old alike, were an intolerable embarrassment, and until the American military withdrawal, Japan, and Hiroshima in particular, had to stifle the need to cry out about their suffering. The statue movement arose just as those suppressed feelings of sorrow, outrage, and bereavement were rising to the surface.

The hideous carnage of the atomic bombings, following years of bloodshed and hunger before and during World War II, gave birth to a steadily growing peace movement in Japan. An American hydrogen-bomb test at the Bikini Atoll in 1954 exposed a crew of Japanese fishermen 130 kilometers east of the test site to fallout and triggered a tremendous public outcry. This outcry was amplified six months later when one of the fishermen died from radiation sickness. Extensive media coverage spread awareness of the chilling effects of radiation, the threat of nuclear weapons, and the damage done in Hiroshima and Nagasaki.

At around the same time, the nation was shocked by an ominous jump in the incidence of juvenile leukemia in those two cities. By the time a group of Hiroshima students and teachers were seeking help to build a statue for these children, thousands of people around the country were grateful for a way to express their sympathy and submit their plea for an end to the suffering of war.

As the group in Hiroshima sought donations for the statue,

they sent fliers all over the country powerfully describing the valiant Sadako folding her paper cranes right up to her death. This publicity connected paper cranes to Sadako, to suffering, and finally, to peace in the minds of the Japanese, and the idea continues to spread throughout the world.

After *Children of the Paper Crane* was published, Sadako's family and classmates, Nomura, and Kawamoto all praised it as the most accurate and detailed of the books that tell the story. Nasu's version not only offers readers the clearest image of the girl who connected paper cranes to peace, it is the first to tell the story of a highly successful grass-roots movement without shying away from the movement's darker side. Above all, this children's author relays with deep empathy the forgotten voices of the children describing their struggle to cope with the mighty movement they had launched.

The Statue for the Children of the A-bomb still stands in Hiroshima Peace Memorial Park, millions of multicolored paper cranes draping its base. The cranes come from various places in Japan, and from Australia, Canada, East Germany, New Zealand, Sweden, the United States—the list goes on and on—but the overwhelming majority are folded by children. The world has found a new symbol of peace, one that transcends language and all the other barriers that divide us, one that is directed toward, identified with, and springs from children—those who hold the future in their hands. For this we can thank Sadako Sasaki, her loving classmates, and the many others who gave of themselves to build a Statue for the Children of the A-bomb.

Part I

1

Field Day

I

Dawn in Hiroshima breaks to the clacking of streetcars. The city is drawn from night's slumber by the sound of steel wheels on rails set in cobblestones, running down the center of the street.

That morning the sound of a streetcar woke Sadako Sasaki too. Her house stood along the Hakushima Line, a hundred meters north of Hatchobori, the city's main shopping district. The three-story structure of wood and mortar trembled slightly in response to the passing streetcars. Sadako's house was near the Kyobashi stop. The trams slowed as they approached. From her third-floor window Sadako could easily see the shuddering car-top poles reaching to the wires above. Now and then small showers of sparks burst from where the poles met the wires, lighting up the tops of the cars in blue-white electric flashes. With the flashes came a crackling sound.

Sadako's mother Fujiko hated those flashes. The sudden

brightness reminded her of the *pika*. But they did not bother Sadako at all. On summer nights she thought she could watch the flashing streetcars forever. She even loved the rumbling.

After the bombing, the Hakushima Line remained closed long after the other city lines were restored to service. In June 1952, the line was moved one block east to Teppocho Avenue, and the streetcars started running. Sadako had been living with the clickety-clack, clickety-clack ever since. In fact, the grinding of the wheels and the trembling of her house were so much a part of daily life that they did not usually wake her up. This particular morning she woke at the sound of the very first car, probably because she was nervous.

She rose quietly and drew back the curtain. Though the sky was still covered by thick clouds, the rain had stopped. When she opened the window slightly, a damp wind blew into the room.

"Is it morning already?" It was the groggy voice of her little sister Mitsue who had been sleeping next to her.

"The rain's stopped, Mit-chan. We'll have Field Day today for sure."

"Really? Good. What time is it?"

"It's only five. Let's get some more sleep."

Sadako quickly closed the window and crawled back into bed. The long-awaited Field Day should have been yesterday. Now she was sure it would not be called off again. She squirmed in her bed, practicing the movements of a baton pass.

"Let's see . . . stretch my right arm behind to receive, then hand it over with my left like this. . . ." Sadako was on the relay team for the sixth-grade Bamboo class. She was the girls' anchor. Mitsue, a second-grader, was already breathing the soft sounds of sleep.

"I have to get some sleep, too." Sadako closed her eyes. It was Monday, October 4, 1954.

II

The weather cleared as the sun rose. Here and there puddles on the field sparkled as bright rays of sunlight broke through the clouds. Teachers and children were going from puddle to puddle, filling them with sand.

9:00 A.M. The Grand Field Day at Noboricho Municipal Elementary School began as scheduled. The rain on Sunday had pushed the meet to a weekday, reducing the number of parents on hand. Perhaps because there were so few spectators, the afternoon's events began without much excitement, even among the children. For the past few years at Noboricho, individual classes were randomly split and assigned to the Red and White teams. As a result, the children were only mildly interested in winning points for the Red or White. Their true competitive spirit was focused on the interclass relays held at the end of the program.

The sixth-graders of the Bamboo class were almost obsessed with this relay. Half a year earlier, during the spring meet in May, the Bamboos had placed a spectacular last. Since then, everyone in the class had been practicing. And not just the fast runners—even the boy with polio had been working out. Now it was almost time to show what their daily training had done.

As the afternoon program proceeded, the Bamboos became more and more fidgety, and Sadako was as nervous as any. When the fifth-grade boys had finished their *kibasen* (mock battle), children wearing official caller ribbons ran in front of the tents, shouting through a megaphone, "Calling all runners for the interclass relay!"

"Let's go, Sada-chan." Tomiko Yokota, who had been sitting next to her, jumped up and brushed off the seat of her bloomers. Sadako got up without speaking.

The rest of the class called out their encouragement as the runners rose.

"Go get 'em!"

"Just don't lose to Wisteria!"

Suddenly feeling embarrassed, Sadako ran behind the spectators' seats as if to escape. The adults were standing and watching from behind where the children sat.

"Hey . . . you're gonna run, aren't you?"

Turning around, Sadako saw her little brother Eiji holding their mother's hand. Fujiko must have come straight from the barbershop; she was still in her white workclothes, looking plump and jovial. Eiji, six years younger than Sadako, was looking up at her.

"Yeah, you cheer for me, OK?"

Fujiko's shining eyes beamed even brighter as she gave her daughter a nod. Sadako nodded back and ran after Tomiko. There were already quite a few contestants at the main gate. From first grade to sixth, every class in each grade sent ten runners to the relays. The lower grades had already begun their races.

"I have to go to the bathroom," Sadako whispered.

Tomiko, sitting nearby, rolled her eyes.

"Again? Didn't you just go?"

"But Mr. Nomura said we should go before we run, didn't he?"

"Yeah, that's right. I guess I'll go with you." They stood up together.

Tomiko and Sadako had been in the same class since second grade. Their families both ran shops, so they came from similar homes. In sports they were great rivals. They were the only two girls in the Bamboo class who could vault to the seventh level of the box horse.

The fifth-grade relay was over. It was time for the sixth-graders. Each team had five boys and five girls. The boys and girls would run alternate laps. The first runner for the Bamboo team was a tall girl, Hiroko Nejime. Her classic, oval face was slightly flushed as she approached the starting line. Six runners, one each from the Pine, Bamboo, Plum, Cherry, Paulownia, and Wisteria classes, placed their hands carefully on the track as they took their positions.

". . . Get set . . ."

They raised their hips at the sound of the teacher's voice. When the pistol cracked, six runners lunged forward as one. Cheering and applause from the spectators rose like a wave, following the runners around the track. At around fifty meters, the pack began to break up. By the time a straining Hiroko passed her baton, she was in second place.

Waiting for her turn, Sadako watched every movement of the runners. She was by far the fastest of the girls. Even among the boys, her only equal was Masatoshi Tasaka, the boys' anchor. Tadaaki Ishimi, who had received the baton from Hiroko, was moving up on the lead runner, a Wisteria. The Wisterias were definitely the ones to beat. They had won easily at the Little Field Day last spring; but by the time Tadaaki came charging down the straight stretch in front of the guest seats to pass the baton to Harumi Yamagata, he had pulled out in front. Long-legged Harumi's smooth pace widened the gap between the Bamboos and the Wisterias. Hideaki Mito, Kikue Itadani, Takashi Kajikawa, and Sadako's best friend Tomiko, all ran with total abandon, burning to make their half-year of hard training pay off. The baton pass they had botched so often during the spring meet was perfect every time today.

Then it was Sadako's turn to wait at the line. She watched as Nobuhiko Jigo came around the wide bend and bounded toward her. Thick eyebrows raised over wide eyes, he ran with his unmistakeable bouncing gait. Sadako ran two or three steps to warm up. She waited. Nobuhiko slammed the red baton into her right hand just as she grabbed for it. She pulled it in close and took off down the white line at full tilt.

The damp earth felt smooth and cool under her bare feet. Her nickname "Monkey" seemed perfect for this girl who ran as if she were leaping through space. The runners behind her, her mother and brother watching from somewhere—everything seemed to vanish. There was only the white line drawing her along, faster and faster.

At the far end of the long curve she could see anchor Masatoshi Tasaka lined up with the other boys. His face danced at the edge of her vision. Her left hand lowered the baton to his in a wide arc. Watching him take off out of the corner of her eye, she veered off the track onto the field. Her heart still pounding at full speed, she gasped deeply as sweat oozed from every pore.

"Sada-chan, I can't believe it. Look! Look, we won!" Tomiko came over to hug her just as Masatoshi broke the tape half a lap ahead of the runner-up.

"We did it! Bamboo's number one!" Nobuhiko and Tadaaki were jumping for joy while the shrieking girl runners joined hands. Two pistol shots signaled the end of the race. The order at the finish was Bamboo, Paulownia, Wisteria, Cherry, Pine, Plum.

The runners returned to their seats to find their waiting classmates even more excited.

"I still say you run weird," said Nobuhiko's twin brother Naohiko. They were almost identical in face and build, but little brother Nobuhiko was more athletic, and Naohiko coached him like a big brother.

"Yeah? Was I bouncing again? I was trying not to. Anyway, so what? It's not like anyone passed me up!"

"Nobu's right. The main thing is, we won! Look at those Wisterias. They been goin' around braggin' all over the place. We won't hear a peep out of 'em now. Even Paulownia wiped 'em out." Toshio Yasui, the Bamboo's comedian, aimed this barb loudly at the Wisteria runners who were just walking off. The Grand Field Day was over.

The sky was now completely clear, and a cold wind blew against the children's bare legs. After each student was given a pencil for participating, the younger children were cleared off the field while the upper grades started to clean up.

"Everyone over here for pictures of the relay team." Mr. Nomura, the Bamboos' teacher, was herding students as he readied the bellows camera that hung constantly from his shoulder. He had found it in a secondhand store when he moved to Hiroshima that spring, and he was always ready to snap photos of his students. "What's the trouble? Line up. Girls in front, boys in back!" Mr. Nomura was shouting, but the children were so used to his raised voice that it never really frightened them.

"He said, 'Girls in front.' Come on. Hurry up and sit down," Takashi said lightly. In choosing who would sit in the middle, the girls were busy backing out in favor of each other.

"Well, if you're gonna argue about it, put Monkey in the middle. She's the fastest," chuckled Nobuhiko.

Hearing her nickname "Monkey," Sadako turned and threw a slight scowl at Nobuhiko.

"Okay, hold it."

Though the children were squinting directly into the late afternoon sun, they still stared intently into the camera. At the light click of the shutter, they relaxed and continued to talk. Mr. Nomura's voice quieted the chatter. "Ladies and gentlemen, you were great today," he said. He looked at them each in turn. "Now you know there's nothing you can't do when you're united. The last team in the spring has suddenly turned up number one. That comes from unity."

The faces turned toward him were unusually meek. That word, "unity"—since April he had preached it at them enough to put calluses on their ears. Today it resonated with fresh meaning.

"Yeah, it's like a dream," Sadako whispered to herself. There they were, the same class that had finished last in the spring meet. She had anchored that team too, but had been unable to pass a single person. And today she had run far in front, she had been virtually running alone.

"Okay, back to clean-up." This time Mr. Nomura's voice scattered the group around the field. Broom-wielding children raised clouds of dust that hung over the track.

III

Tsuyoshi Nomura, teacher of the sixth-grade Bamboo class, was born in Taiwan, which was a Japanese colony at the time of his birth. His birthday was January 1, 1926, which made him twenty-eight on the day of the race. When the Second World War ended, he came back to Japan and started teaching in Miyoshi, Hiroshima Prefecture, his father's hometown. He had been transferred to Noboricho Elementary School in Hiroshima City the previous April. The Bamboos were his first class there.

Coming from a tiny school in the mountains where he and his students had felt like a family, Mr. Nomura found everything about this city school strange. The Bamboo class had a total of sixty-two pupils—thirty-four boys and twenty-eight girls. Besides their sheer numbers, Mr. Nomura was amazed by their cliquishness. The kids from each neighborhood stuck together in groups that had "bosses" who fought each other. And, of course, there were times when the fights did not stop at words. After the fights had run their course, it was no easy matter to get back to school work.

"It's like the dark ages in there," he would say, and sometimes there was nothing he could do about it. The rumor that their fifth-grade teacher had thrown up his hands and resigned may have been more than mere talk. Even the other children in the school considered the Bamboos a wild bunch.

Mr. Nomura had come to his new post fresh from his wedding. A newlywed in a new job, he was having a rough time of it. Still, his natural optimism, coupled with his harsh experience in the country school, gave him the resolve to cope with his new roomful of warriors. Compared to his previous assignment, where he had to climb over a mountain just to buy a piece of paper or a pencil, conditions were wonderful in this new place, he kept telling himself. And it was not as though he could not understand why this gang was so wild.

Mr. Nomura was well aware of the atomic bomb, the *pika*. It had exploded in the air over the city nine years earlier on August 6, 1945, killing countless people and wreaking havoc on the lives of the rest. On that day these inner-city children had seen their whole world, including the Noboricho Elementary School District, burned to the ground. In the nine years after Japan's surrender, their town had gradually regained a bustling, prosperous look, but the wounds of war were still obvious. Half of the Bamboos had lost a parent. One boy had lost almost his entire family and was being raised by his grandmother. Even most of those whose parents were healthy had lost at least one family member to the atomic bomb or to the war in general.

Then there were the families who had been brought back from the Asian continent or islands in the south. Noboricho Elementary was so overpopulated now because it had absorbed so many children returning from other countries. Mr. Nomura himself had been swept to the school in the same tide. He understood deep in his bones the pain of the children. Only just married and recently transferred, Mr. Nomura fell right in step with the Bamboos.

Semiannual field days were a long tradition at elementary schools in Hiroshima: the May field day was called the "Little Field Day" or "Flying Carp Field Day"; in autumn was the

"Grand Field Day." The main attraction of field days at Noboricho Elementary was always the class relays run at the end of the day. For these events, each member of the usually fragmented Bamboo class was determined to win. Yet the spring meet had been a disaster. In Hiroshima's slang the word "*kabachi*" meant stuck up and conceited, and it had been an apt description of the Bamboos until they lost the spring relay and were cowed into silence.

Since the beginning of the school year in April, Mr. Nomura had been busy just getting acquainted with his class; but after the race in May, he set about giving them some guidance.

"Don't you feel any shame?" he sneered. "You must. The very last ones. No wonder the other classes are calling you the rags."

Naohiko, till now clenching his teeth, suddenly raised his bent head.

"You don't seem too miserable about it." By nature a kid who hated losing, Naohiko scrapped with his brother a lot, except when Nobuhiko was getting the worst of a fight. Then he would come leaping to his brother's side, no matter how many were on the other side.

"Those who do their best and still lose have a right to talk about feeling miserable. Did you do your best? Well? What do you say?" Mr. Nomura's glasses glinted sharply. "Look at Tasaka, or your brother. They don't look slow to me. The girls either. Sasaki's as fast as a boy. So why did we lose today?"

"We kept losing the baton on the passes," muttered Yoshihiro Ooka, leader of the Motomachi pack.

"Ah, yes. There was that. In a relay it isn't just how fast you can move yourself. You need teamwork. Am I right?" He gazed slowly around the classroom as he spoke.

Yoshiko Hattori spoke up in a timid voice, "What can we do about teamwork?"

"It's up to you to think about that. I wash my hands of it." As he replied, Mr. Nomura turned his gaze out the window. The May sun streamed into the second story of the wooden school building.

One girl asked, "Shouldn't we practice real hard?" Mr. Nomura remained absorbed in staring out the window.

When he heard a voice say, "I think we should practice every day between now and the fall field day," Mr. Nomura nodded in his heart and thought, That must be Shinichiro Hayashi.

"Hey, listen. Will it just be the runners who practice?" asked Shinji Miyasako in his high, easy-going voice.

"Idiot! Everyone practices, even the slowest people in the class," retorted Ken Hosokawa as shouts of "Yeah" and "That's right" from around the room backed him up.

Masako Yamaguchi asked uneasily, "When do we practice? After class?" Since her father was dead and her mother worked, Masako had to do almost all the housework herself. Her grandfather, an ex-military man, was at home, but instead of helping her, he constantly nagged her about her chores. She always had to fly straight home after school.

"After school, during lunch, it doesn't matter as long as it's every day."

Then a small voice asked, "Um, is it okay if I practice, too?" It was Ikuo Shishido. Mr. Nomura could barely keep from turning around. Ikuo's legs had been crippled by polio. He could get around, but he certainly could not run.

No sooner had the classroom fallen into a shocked stillness than Nobuhiko Jigo's cheerful voice rang out, "Sure, make Donchan practice, too. We already said everyone would run, didn't we?"

"All right!" Everyone cheered and broke into applause.

Mr. Nomura once more gazed slowly around the classroom. "Have you pea brains come up with anything?"

IV

That had been six months ago. The Bamboos were as wild as ever. The other classes still called them rags behind their backs, but somehow the relay practicing went on. When classes let out, they automatically gathered at the schoolyard for warm-ups, two laps around the field and baton-passing practice, no matter how rainy or windy it was.

Mr. Nomura joined them when he could. His mountain school experience had taught him how basic to education it was to be close to the kids and to exercise along with them. While he trained with them, he talked constantly about unity.

Each one of those sixty-two children came from a different type of family and had different abilities in school work. Still, here they were, plopped down together in this class, and nothing could change that. Mr. Nomura wanted them to develop bonds that would keep them together even into adulthood. He often invited them to his home on the edge of Yoshijima-cho in the southern part of the city. Near his house was a huge open space that had been the Japanese military airport, and beyond the airport lay the blue expanse of Hiroshima Bay.

On most Sundays the children would walk for almost an hour to get to his house. They gathered on the grassy plain of the old airport and played tag or dug for shells on the beach. Although lunch was usually just steamed sweet potatoes prepared by Mr. Nomura's wife, the students fell on them gratefully. For some reason Mr. Nomura felt shy about having his students know that the woman in his house was his wife, so he told them she was his younger sister. Behind his rough pose he was like a bashful schoolboy himself.

Mr. Nomura put physical exercise (and especially the relay) first, but his specialty was biology. When they dissected frogs during science class, he had the children bury the frogs afterward to teach them consideration for the lives they had taken.

Mr. Nomura cared for his pupils in many ways. Motomachi was a part of the school district that used to be almost entirely devoted to various military installations. After the war, hastily built public housing and illegal shacks were thrown up everywhere. These houses were tiny, and the children who came from them had no place to study. Mr. Nomura went out of his way to give these kids special help. Eventually, like water soaking into dry ground, his hard work softened the children's hearts. There was no doubt that this man's patient leadership was behind the amazing success of the Bamboos in the fall relay. Still, no one could have predicted that in later years this class of "rags" would ignite the movement that led to the erection of the "Statue for the Children of the A-bomb." And the one who would become the central focus of that movement, Sadako Sasaki, had not the slightest clue about her fate.

2

The Time of Her Life

I

Sadako's parents ran a barbershop. Her father, Shigeo, was thirty-nine, born in 1915. Her mother, Fujiko, was thirty-six. They had four children: Sadako, her older brother Masahiro, who was in seventh grade at Noboricho Junior High School, second-grader Mitsue, and five-year-old Eiji.

Mr. Sasaki was a craftsman who took his work seriously. He had been managing his business in Hiroshima since before the war, and when he was drafted to be a soldier, his wife and sister Chizuko kept things running smoothly while he was away. After their house was destroyed by the A-bombing, they moved to Kamikawatachi-cho in Miyoshi City, Mrs. Sasaki's ancestral home. Two years later, in 1947, they opened up shop again downtown in what is now Teppo-cho.

With six chairs for customers, several employees, and a central location, the shop did a reasonably good business, but sometime around the summer of 1954, a dark shadow began to envelop the

Sasaki family. An acquaintance who had borrowed money using Mr. Sasaki as a guarantor became unable to pay his debt, and the responsibility fell to Mr. Sasaki. Although he always disciplined his children strictly, Shigeo Sasaki was soft-hearted toward others, which turned out to be a great mistake in this case. By the end of that summer, the bill collector came regularly to the shop to demand payment. Mr. Sasaki frequently slipped out on money-raising errands, but both he and his wife tried to shelter their children from these troubles.

Except for this one money problem, the Sasaki family was doing quite well. The children were lively and helped with the housework. Sadako especially was very dependable. Although she had never been particularly talkative or outgoing, she had also never been gloomy; she cheerfully helped care for her younger brother and sister.

Perhaps because both parents worked and Sadako, as the oldest daughter, had been used to caring for the younger children, she somehow seemed older than her classmates. Her way of gently and quietly doing what had to be done might have been inherited from her mother. Her father was more demanding, insisting that the children clean the barbershop as well as finish the housework before they could play. He would scold them even about keeping the shoes arranged neatly in their doorway and stacking their futon carefully. But Mrs. Sasaki went about her tasks silently and methodically. She rarely raised her voice with her children and was more apt to wait on customers with smiles than with words.

Compared to Sadako, Masahiro Sasaki, her older brother, was outgoing and open. He was more absorbed with school life than with family. Since little Mitsue and Eiji tired easily of everyday chores and depended on help with everything, Sadako would take over for them, with a soothing assurance, "Don't worry, don't worry, I'll do it for you." With a father hounded by money troubles and a mother pressed by the family business, middle-born Sadako fell into her role instinctively. It must have been that life of self-discipline that shaped the character of the girl who, suffering with leukemia later, almost never complained about the pain. For now, though, the gentle but boyishly athletic Sadako was unaware of the disease that was readying its attack. She was enjoying every day.

Sadako had started in Noboricho Elementary in April 1949. Her early birthday—January 7—had placed her in a higher grade, with those born in 1942. Average weight, average height, slightly dark skin, a fairly ordinary face with large, round eyes— she looked like a lot of other girls. Nor was she one of the great intellects in the class. Her favorite subject was music, but only because she was crazy about popular singer Hibari Misora, whose tunes she liked to hum.

Sadako's life changed when she entered Mr. Nomura's sixth-grade class. Because of the teacher's effort to build group feeling by practicing for the relay, runners with fast, powerful legs started to receive a lot of attention in the Bamboo class. Besides running, Mr. Nomura energetically herded his students through exercises on the box horse, the horizontal bar, and the tumbling mat. Sadako was one of those who generally had kept to the shadows, but now she took to gym class like a fish to water.

Sadako, who had never before had a word to say about school, confided to her mother in May, "Our new teacher is strict but he's fun—I like going to school now."

When her classmates stuck her with the nickname "Monkey," it had less to do with her personality, which was placid, than with their amazed respect for her nimble, fast legs. Nobuhiko hated to run against her. Strain as he might, she always came from behind and sped past him. The usually mild-mannered girl would breathe "Heh, heh, heh" in his direction as she overtook him. Nobuhiko was no quitter, but even Sadako's back seemed to be laughing at him as he pushed on, red-faced and desperate, into the widening distance between them.

Hurling his cap on the ground, he would cry out afterward, "I'm not running against that!"

Had she been anyone else, Nobuhiko might have picked a fight with her, saying, "What were you laughing at?" He might even have lost his temper and hit her. But somehow he just could not feel like fighting with Sadako. Not only was she usually quiet and gentle, but she had an air of maturity that held him back.

Sadako's friends were Tomiko Yokota, who had been in her class since they were small; Masako Yamaguchi, who lived near her; Kazuko Hikiji; and Atsuko Nomura. But they were not a set group who always played together. Cleaning up after breakfast every morning left Sadako just enough time to slip into her seat before the bell, so she had no special friend for walking to school. In school she could play easily with anyone, a trait she might have gotten from her father.

During the second semester she was voted P.E. teacher's aide, not only because she was good in P.E., but because both boys and girls liked her. Sadako's election over students with higher grades was a sign that the class was absorbing Mr. Nomura's belief that ability cannot be evaluated merely by grades, that class positions should be filled on the basis of character and personality. Under Mr. Nomura's leadership, the ragged Bamboos were slowly shifting and changing. Winning the fall relay gave them all, Sadako included, a surge of courage and self-confidence. These days shone with a special brilliance in Sadako's brief life.

II

Every year toward the end of November, downtown Hiroshima was crowded with revelers at the Ebisu Festival. Shintenchi,

Kinzagai, Horikawacho, Hondori, and all the shop-covered streets around Ebisucho, where the Ebisu Shrine stands, held the "Ebisuko Big Sale"—discount sales that began well before the festival each year. More on account of the big sale than the festival itself, people flocked there from all over the city as well as from the surrounding areas day after day.

It was almost ten years after Japan's defeat in the Second World War, and her people were looking toward a new age. The Korean War had revived the stagnated economy; people anticipated a change for the better. In fact, this was the beginning of the period of spectacular growth that came to be known as the "Jinmu Boom."

At the same time, however, despite a constitutional prohibition against the creation of military forces, Japan established a defense agency. The "National Police Reserve," established under orders from the Allied Forces Headquarters (GHQ) at the time of the Korean War, was renamed the "Peace Preservation Corps," and then the "Self-Defense Forces." Local police forces were unified into a single national police force. Two laws governing education were established to prohibit teachers from participating in political activities. Japan, a country of peace and democracy, was changing her national policies in compliance with a military agreement called the U.S.-Japan Security Treaty.

Nine years after the atomic bombing, the so-called atomic desert of Hiroshima was changing tremendously. Road repairs begun in 1952 were progressing smoothly, and the expansion of the streetcar line between Inarimachi and Tokaichi had just been completed.

Hondori Street had become an arcade filled with stores, attracting even more shoppers. But while reconstruction had turned crude, asphalted roads into nicely paved avenues, the atomic bombing had not become a thing of the past to the people who lived in Hiroshima. Now and then one would hear talk of the bombing among middle-aged women riding the street cars, among junior high students in classrooms, or at workplaces. Without fail people were still asking each other: "Where were you when the *pika* hit?"

It is hard to say just when the words *"pika"* and *"pika don"* came to mean the atomic bomb. The words "atomic bomb" or "A-bomb" were largely unknown in Hiroshima at the time of the bombing. And no one who had been there could forget the paralyzing flash (*"pika"*) followed by the roaring blast (*"don"*). For them, these were the words that fit that moment best. The phrase "A-bomb" did not come naturally to the lips in daily conversation.

The idea of a nuclear bombing is intrinsically abnormal. For most of the human race it is the ultimate abnormality. Yet, in Hiroshima the abnormal had become normal, and nine years later the bombing still sat heavily in the midst of everyday life.

Just as the word *"pika"* persisted in daily conversation, the effects of the *pika* lay like a shadow on individual lives. One did not have to go down to the "A-bomb Memorial Collection" to see the scars of the *pika*. Human bones were still continually being unearthed at construction sites. Glass bottles, twisted and gnarled like candy, lay scattered on the riverbeds along with blistered rooftiles. Reddish-black burn scars glared on the bright, smiling cheeks of young women walking around town and on the backs of laborers in the relief program for the unemployed.

Under the eaves of houses hung with the sign "In Mourning" for the death of a family member, the conversations of old people recycled the same familiar phrases.

"Just as we thought. It was the *pika*, wasn't it?"

"No help for that. There's no cure."

In Hiroshima, located in the temperate Inland Sea area, winter winds do not begin to blow until after the Ebisu Festival in mid-

November. The Ebisu Festival is the signal for people to get out their *kotatsu* (heater tables). Around this time Sadako Sasaki caught a cold. There was no real fever, nothing to keep her home from school or dampen her spirits, just a swollen and stiff lymph node under her left ear. Since she seemed perfectly healthy, her parents paid little attention to this. But deep within her body, an irrevocable change had taken place.

Sunday, December 12, with winter vacation approaching, Sadako went with a few friends to Mr. Nomura's house. Unlike most of the others, she had rarely been there before because her father's barbershop stayed open on Sundays. That day nearly twenty boys and girls appeared at the Nomura home. They played their usual game of tag on the grounds of the former airport; in dry grass that hid them up to their necks, they sorted into "allies" and "enemies" and chased each other.

Sadako was unusually active; in fact she was a little rough. Spotting an enemy boy through the dry grass, she sped after him and lunged into a ferocious tackle. When she pursued Yuzo Yamane—known to be a bit of a coward—he let out a shriek as he dashed off.

"Hey, Sasaki? What's the matter?" asked Mr. Nomura, when he noticed her resting. Sitting with her legs stretched out on the dry grass, shoulders heaving, Sadako raised her head. "You're awfully energetic today, aren't you?"

The girl showed her teeth in a little grin.

"*Sensei*—Teacher—Sasaki-san caught six boys all by herself," boasted Atsuko Nomura, as if it were her own achievment.

"Really, if Sada-chan were here, we'd win every time. Come next time too, okay Sada-chan?" chimed in Yoshiko Hattori.

Sadako spoke up. "I didn't know it was this much fun. Bring me again, okay?" Her rest over, she began dashing about like a crazy thing, as if she were trying to shake something off. Watching her, Mr. Nomura had an ominous premonition. At dusk, as he looked at the receding shadows of the children heading home in groups, he felt, for some reason, that Sadako's shadow was lighter than the rest, and he found himself calling her name.

Her braided hair whipped around as she turned her inquiring face toward him.

"Nothing. Take care going home, okay?"

He wanted to say something else, but just nodded. Maybe there's something wrong with the family business, he told himself, to silence his worry about her behavior. This was the last day that Sadako would ever visit her teacher and play on the old airfield.

Right after the start of winter vacation, Sadako complained to her mother, "Look, there's a kind of bump on my neck."

"Where?" asked her mother, feeling her neck. There was definitely a swelling on the left side. "Could it be the mumps?" she wondered. But Sadako's forehead felt normal.

Later Fujiko mentioned it to her husband. "Shigeo, there's a swelling on the side of Sadako's neck."

"Hmm, does she have a fever?"

"No, but she does look a little thin."

"Well, I hope it's nothing serious," he said, his eyes intent on his ledger while his right hand deftly flicked the beads on the abacus. He had to raise a certain amount of money by New Year's Eve. He had paid off the original loan by taking out another. Now that one had to be paid off by taking out a third. As the Sasaki family continued around this vicious circle, their finances became ever more desperate.

Mr. Sasaki took off his glasses and rubbed the points between his eyes where the glasses had touched. He had lost weight and his hair was thinning. Seeing her husband like this, Mrs. Sasaki hesitated to talk any more about Sadako's health.

"Let's take the children to the country for New Year's," she suggested brightly. "Maybe it'll help Sadako get better."

"Yeah, let's do that," her husband answered with a light nod. Suddenly, as if wrung from a place deep inside, a heavy sigh escaped him.

III

On New Year's Day, 1955, Mrs. Sasaki set out with her children for her family home, Kamikawatachi-cho, in Miyoshi City, two hours from Hiroshima Station on the National Railway's Geibi Line. The mountains were covered with snow, a thrill for children reared on the relatively snowless Seto Inland Sea. As soon as they arrived, seventh-grade Masahiro, sixth-grade Sadako, second-grade Mitsue, and five-year-old Eiji were romping in the snow with their cousins.

When the children had all gone out to play, a relative approached Mrs. Sasaki, who was sitting at the *kotatsu* in the living room.

"Listen, Fujiko, isn't Sadako's lymph gland swollen?"

"Yes, since the end of the year. And she has definitely already had the mumps."

"But listen, . . ." continued the woman, lowering her voice. From the other side of the bright *shoji*, the translucent, sliding paper doors, came the voices of the children struggling to fly a kite. "I don't want to upset you, but couldn't it be her lungs?"

"Her lungs?"

"When you get tuberculosis, your lymph glands swell. She looks pale too."

"It couldn't be. . . ."

"No, it probably isn't, but you should have her checked by a doctor."

Just then the *shoji* shot open and a sobbing Eiji burst in on them. Throwing himself on his mother's back he whined, "Mitsue was mean to me!"

From outside, they could hear Sadako's bright voice calling, "Ei-chan, come here, I'll make you a snowman."

Mrs. Sasaki shot a look at her relative that meant "Tuberculosis? A lively child like that?" But during the train ride home, Fujiko's thoughts that "It couldn't be" turned into "What if . . ."

When the New Year's holiday ended, Mrs. Sasaki took Sadako to a local surgical clinic. The doctor, an accommodating man, was willing to perform brief physical examinations as well as surgery. Treating Sadako's lump as a viral infection, he injected her with antibiotics, but the shot had no effect. After four treatments, Sadako's parents naturally began to grow more worried.

Among the customers at the barbershop was a pediatrician. Increasingly bewildered by Sadako's situation, Mr. Sasaki next took his daughter to this customer's clinic at Sakancho. The doctor examined her with great care, and then seemed absorbed in thought for some time before he said slowly, "Would you be willing to take Sadako to the ABCC for a more complete examination?"

"To the ABCC?" repeated Mr. Sasaki, as though he had not heard clearly.

"Sada-chan was exposed to the A-bomb, wasn't she? Please, just to make sure that it's not related to that," the doctor explained, dropping his eyes to her chart.

"Doctor, she gets checked at the ABCC every two years. She was just in last June and they didn't find anything wrong at all."

"Yes, it's very unlikely, but just in case," he said, looking suddenly toward the girl, as if he had just remembered that she was there. "You're growing up. You'll be a fine young woman soon."

Sadako giggled softly. But when the doctor turned back to her father, the forceful tone of his voice was unmistakable. "You'll take her, won't you."

After the war, the name ABCC and the image of its conspicuous, wood-paneled station wagons were etched in the minds of everyone who lived in Hiroshima. The initials stood for Atomic Bomb Casualty Commission. Established in both Hiroshima and Nagasaki in November 1946 by order of the U.S. president, the ABCC was created to study the late effects of the two bombings. At first it was only a room rented from the Red Cross Hospital, but by 1947 it had moved to a building in Ujina. In 1951 it moved to the top of Hijiyama Hill, with seven barracks that looked like half-barrels sliced the long way. Supposedly a cooperative venture between the two countries, the ABCC was so heavily funded and controlled by the United States that the people of Hiroshima saw it as an organ of the U.S. military and definitely had no good impression of it.

There were many reasons to distrust the ABCC. For one, during the seven years after the war when Japan was under U.S. occupation, the American government confiscated all public or private studies of the bombing effects conducted by Japanese, and banned all Japanese publications related to the bombing. Military regulations maintained such tight control over the population that even personal accounts of individual experiences and poetry about the bombing were silenced. By controlling the press, the occupation government not only undermined all scientific efforts to study the destruction caused by the bomb, but also slowed the provision of adequate medical care. Even today, the lives of atomic bomb victims are endangered because of the delay in creating a proper medical care system.

This policy of covering up the A-bomb meant that the ABCC was the only organ authorized to conduct research or publish material about the bombing. The outside world was led to believe that only the ABCC could present the truth about the bombing. How closely the ABCC was actually connected to the military, whether or not its purpose was to conduct research necessary for the next nuclear war, it was impossible to say. One thing was clear: it was not established to help the survivors of the bombing.

Reportedly, over 90 percent of the survivors were studied by the commission but not one of them was offered even the slightest medical treatment. The ABCC physicians sampled the survivors' blood, cut samples of their tissue for cell-structure analysis, and studied their bodily systems, but they did not follow up any of these examinations with medicine, surgery, or hospitalization. The flashy ABCC station wagons would pull up at survivors' homes, load up the bedridden in stretchers, and transport them to the Hijiyama research center, where they were subjected to the most minute examinations and then simply trundled home again.

It is not hard, considering how they were treated, to imagine how the survivors felt about the ABCC. They were the guinea pigs, the specimens to satisfy the military's desire to learn everything they could about the effects of the bomb. By 1955, the Allied Forces had withdrawn from Japan, and the ABCC was trying to soften its image in Hiroshima, but hostility died hard. Also by this time, the ABCC was interested in studying second-generation victims, the children of the survivors. The sight of the easily recognizable station wagons arriving at schools to whisk children off was becoming familiar.

Sadako was no stranger to the half-barrel-shaped buildings on Hijiyama Hill. Every two years, around her birthday, she was presented for study. First, they made her take off everything, even her underwear. Then they put her in a short, white robe, took her blood, and did an electrocardiogram and an x-ray. They sometimes had her climb on and off a chair while they studied the condition of her heart.

During her checkup in June of the previous year, 1954, nothing had been wrong with her blood.

This time, following the pediatrician's instructions, Sadako visited the ABCC on January 28 and again on February 16. Both times her body was studied as never before. During the second exam, they even checked the fluid of her bone marrow.

They had her bend over like a shrimp and pierced her hipbone with a needle; it was a painful procedure that makes even adult men groan. Twelve-year-old Sadako was always slow to tears, but she cried out loud during this test.

Out in the corridor, Sadako's parents could hear their daughter's cries. Unable to stand it anymore, Mrs. Sasaki grabbed her husband's arm. "Shigeo, it's too cruel! We can't make her go through this. Let's get her out of here." He responded to the entreaty in her face by silently pressing her hand.

Even on the days when she had to go to the ABCC for these physical examinations, Sadako went to school first. After morning classes she went straight to the ABCC, still clutching her satchel. She was proud that she had never missed a day of school in her life, but by February, she had to sit out and watch during gym.

In gym, and after school as well, the Bamboos continued to practice the relay. With graduation just ahead, there would be no more field days for them, but they were still out on the field, silently passing the baton and running in the cold wind.

The day after Sadako's second trip to the ABCC, Fumiko Yamamoto called to her out on the schoolyard. "Sada-chan, where were you? Is something wrong?"

Sadako pointed to the bandage on her neck, saying "My neck is swollen so I had to go to the doctor at the ABCC."

"Really?" Staring at Sadako's neck, she thought it did seem to be bulging.

"I hate the ABCC!" Sadako exploded, spewing out the words. "They make you take off all your clothes. Then they stick a needle in the very bottom of your hipbone."

Fumiko had been overseas and had not returned to Hiroshima until after the war was over; she had no special feeling about the ABCC, but she was squeamish and recoiled at Sadako's description. "How awful! You have to get naked? I'm glad I wasn't in Hiroshima during the *pika*."

Neither Fumiko nor even Sadako thought there was anything special connecting them to that bombing, so faint in memory, so far off in time.

IV

On February 18, after Sadako had gone to school as usual, her parents received a phone call sometime after 9:00 A.M. from the pediatrician who had examined her. "The results of Sadako's examination at the ABCC are back. We can't discuss it over the phone, so can you come down here, Mr. Sasaki?" The doctor's voice sounded somewhat strained. Changing out of his work-clothes and hurrying into his overcoat, Mr. Sasaki walked out of the house. It was a clear, cold, windy day.

As soon as he entered the clinic, he was whisked back to the examination room where the doctor sat with folded arms behind a big desk covered with papers. With a swift glance, Mr. Sasaki saw the English letters ABCC printed along with the logo at the top of the pages. "Doctor, does Sadako have something bad?" he burst out.

The doctor turned toward him slowly. "Sada-chan was ex-posed to the bomb at Kusunokicho, wasn't she?"

"Yes, when she was two."

"Hmm," he said, with a big sigh. "Since you're her father, I'll be perfectly frank with you. There's something unusual about her white blood corpuscles."

"That's something in her blood, right? Why would there be something wrong with her blood?"

"Well . . ."

"Doctor, please talk so I can understand. Is it something very complicated?"

"Not so complicated, but it is life-threatening. The way it's progressing now, she may not last another half a year."

For a second Mr. Sasaki's vision went blank. Then he realized the doctor was still staring at him.

"Mr. Sasaki, please get her to the Red Cross Hospital as soon as possible. I'll arrange it with them."

Mr. Sasaki finally found his voice. "Doctor, is she sick from the bomb? They say you don't get well from A-bomb disease." His mind had been swept empty, but at the edge of his awareness the doctor's words resounded.

"That's certainly not true. If she gets treatment from a hospital with the right equipment, she may live for one or two years. What's going to happen if you give up right from the beginning?"

Sadako has A-bomb disease. Sadako has A-bomb disease. Even after he walked out of the clinic into the cold air, Shigeo Sasaki did not think to put on his coat.

At that time all after-effects and late effects related to the bombing were called "A-bomb disease" or "atomic disease" or "Hiroshima disease." Mr. Sasaki knew many people who had died of the A-bomb or who were suffering some effects from it. The symptoms were all different, but the survivors had one thing in common: once they came down with something, they never completely recovered. Even if they did not contract a specific disease, something was always not working right. They caught frequent colds. Or they tired easily. Their wounds got infected more often and healed more slowly. Mr. Sasaki walked blindly, his mind full. He finally arrived at his home where he spoke to his wife.

"Fujiko, Sadako has something wrong with her white blood cells because of the *pika*. At the rate it's going now, she won't last more than another half a year."

"It must be some kind of mistake," Sadako's mother said, her mind suddenly blank. "A healthy girl like that."

"That's what the doctor said. I think we have to believe it." He staggered to his feet again.

"Shigeo, where are you going?"

"I'm going to school to get her."

His wife stood up too. "Then I want to have a kimono made for her."

"A kimono?"

"Yes. If she has A-bomb disease, at least I want her to have a pretty kimono. A young girl should have one." Her words were choked by tears.

"You're right. We've never given her a kimono," said her father. "We'll stop at the shop on the way back and have her fitted." He drew out all the hundred-yen bills in the cash register and put them in his coat pocket. He crossed the wide streetcar street and was soon at the school.

As he entered the gate to the schoolyard he saw a line of students in their gym uniforms. A male teacher in glasses stood with a whistle in his mouth. He recognized that it was Mr. Nomura, so he knew those students were the Bamboos. Shigeo's eyes searched for his daughter and found her standing despondently off to the side on a platform, wearing her regular clothes.

Seeing her there, he lost control of the tears he had been fighting back. Quickly, he removed his glasses and wiped his eyes before setting out across the field.

"Sadako's father is here."

"*Sensei*, Sadako's father is here."

Mr. Nomura turned around and called out, "Mr. Sasaki, can I help you?" The man's strained face told Mr. Nomura that something was wrong. "Okay everyone, I need to talk to Mr. Sasaki. Break time!" He led Mr. Sasaki to the edge of the field. "Sir, is it something to do with your daughter's health?"

"Yes. The doctor gave us the results of the ABCC examination. He says she has A-bomb disease and her white blood cells are abnormal; at this rate she doesn't have more than six months."

"Her white blood cells? No. . . ." Mr. Nomura knew a good bit about A-bomb symptoms, and his biology background told him that a problem with white blood cells meant leukemia or something like it.

A year earlier, 1954, on the first of March, a fishing boat called the *Daigo Fukuryu Maru*, the Lucky Dragon Number 5, from Yaizu, Shizuoka Prefecture, had been caught near the Bikini Atoll during a hydrogen bomb test by the American government. The crew had been exposed to radioactive fallout, the so-called "ashes of death." Aikichi Kuboyama, a forty-year-old crew member, had died of radiation sickness half a year earlier on September 23. As a result of this incident, more people had come to understand the effects of radiation and to recognize the threat of nuclear weapons.

"Sadako-san was exposed to the A-bomb, wasn't she?"

"Yes, at our house at Kusunokicho, when she was only two."

"Oh, I see. What happens now?"

"The doctor wants her to go to the Red Cross Hospital." Shigeo Sasaki's eyes again filled with tears, tears that Sadako must never see. Stealing a glance, he was relieved to see his daughter deep in conversation with Makiko Yamashige. He could even see her laughing at something, enjoying herself, through his tear-clouded glasses.

"So you'll be taking Sadako-san home now?"

"Yes."

"I understand." He turned back toward Sadako casually and called, "Sasaki! Your dad's here to pick you up. Go get your things!" With a suspicious look and a quick nod, she ran toward the schoolhouse.

"*Sensei*," a girl's voice called to Mr. Nomura. "Is Sasaki-san going to the ABCC again?"

Without turning his gaze away from Sadako's back, he answered, "Yeah, something like that. What we need is for her to get well fast and get back into relay practice."

"You can say that again," said Nobuhiko, lightheartedly. "Without Monkey we lose heart. She's our best weapon."

Soon Sadako reappeared with her satchel. She bowed politely and said "Goodbye *sensei*, goodbye everyone," the way students always did at the end of the school day. Mr. Nomura watched father and daughter walk toward the rear exit and turn out of sight.

"*Sensei . . .*"

Startled, Mr. Nomura quickly blew his whistle and yelled, "All right, everyone, one more lap!" Leading the group off, he kept thinking, Sadako has leukemia? It has to be a mistake. But as he ran the last lap, he had to push the thought from his mind over and over again.

V

Sadako noticed that her father headed toward Hatchobori instead of across the streetcar line, "Are we going to the ABCC again?" she asked.

"No, we don't have to go there anymore. Your mother wants to have a kimono made for you, so we're going to have you fitted now."

She blinked unbelievingly a few times and returned quickly, "That's expensive. I don't need a kimono."

"Let the grown-ups worry about money." He grabbed the canvas satchel she was lugging with difficulty and was surprised by how light he found it.

She looked at him suspiciously. Why was he being so nice? "What is it? Has something happened?"

"Yes. You might have to go into the hospital. It looks like that lump on your neck won't get well unless you do."

"Oh . . . go into the hospital . . ."

The two walked on in silence. By the time they had been to the store, picked out a cherry blossom pattern, and returned home, it was after noon.

That night Shigeo and Fujiko Sasaki closed up shop and boarded a train just after 9:00. They rode to Mihara City in the eastern part of the prefecture where Shigeo's sister lived. She was an excellent seamstress and, along with her mother and Fujiko, she spent most of the night sewing Sadako's gaily colored kimono. The next morning they returned to Hiroshima. The thought that her daughter might have A-bomb disease made Fujiko do unusual things.

The next morning Sadako jumped up and danced when she saw her brand-new kimono. "Oh, it's so pretty!"

"Come and put it on." Urged on by her mother, she slid her arm into a sleeve covered with cherry blossoms. "It really suits you." Smiling with satisfaction, her parents studied their daughter in her first kimono.

"No fair," Mitsue complained. "Sadako gets a kimono." "I want a kimono too." Eiji joined in, pouting through full cheeks.

"What are you talking about?" snapped Masahiro. "Sadako's going to the hospital. Is that something to be jealous about?" He was the only one of the three who understood what was happening.

That day, for the first time in her life, Sadako did not go to school. She set out for the City Hospital in Kamiyacho for yet another examination. As long as there was a slight possibility of misdiagnosis, the Sasakis could still hope.

Soon after Sadako had returned home from the City Hospital, the pediatrician telephoned. "All the paperwork is done for Sadako to enter the Red Cross Hospital," he told Shigeo. "Take her there on Monday at 9:00 A.M. Just mention my name and they'll bring out the papers. The Red Cross Hospital has all the best equipment, and they can get medicine from the ABCC. Don't worry too much." Since he was their customer as well as their doctor, he tried to keep his voice cheerful.

After he hung up, Mr. Sasaki said, "It's decided. She'll go into the Red Cross Hospital on Monday."

Fujiko's hand stopped working the clippers on a customer's hair.

"That's over by Senda-machi, isn't it?"

"Yeah, from Kamiyacho you take the streetcar to Ujina for fourteen, fifteen minutes. You need to pack a bag, her nightgown and things."

"How long do you think she'll be in?"

"I don't know. . . ." He stared into the kitchen where he could see Sadako's back as she prepared lunch. They had only just come home from the City Hospital, and already she had found a way to help.

On Saturday afternoon business was hopping as usual. The parents staggered their lunch breaks and had to rush back to work as soon as possible. After she put the lunch things away, Sadako stepped down to the dirt floor doorway, announcing, "I'm going over to school for a little while."

"What? It's Saturday afternoon. There's no one there now."

"But they might be running relays. I want to say goodbye."

"All right," her father said. "I'll go with you. I should say something, too." Mr. Sasaki passed his clippers to one of his employees.

One of his regular customers, partway through a cut, looked at him in the mirror and asked, "Hey, is Sada-chan going on a trip?"

"She's going into the Red Cross Hospital on Monday."

"She is? What's wrong?"

"There's an enlarged lymph gland on her neck."

"Yeah, I see the bandage, but I thought it was a sore throat. Sada-chan, get well fast, okay?" She laughed shyly at his words. No one had yet mentioned white blood cells or A-bomb disease to her.

When they left, Mr. Sasaki wound a scarf around Sadako's neck. The twigs on the roadside trees shook in a northwesterly winter wind. The young sycamore trees that had been planted three years before when the road was widened still looked thin.

Suddenly lifting her face to her father, Sadako said, "The hospital will cost us money, won't it?"

"What are you talking about? All we care about is you getting well. In April you'll be in junior high."

"Yeah, I'll be out of the hospital by then, won't I?"

"You might be out in a week."

"Uh huh. Since I don't hurt anywhere. I don't even have a fever."

She skipped lightly just to show him.

After only one day, Sadako already missed school. As soon as they walked in through the back entrance, the sharp-eyed relay runners ran over to meet them.

"Hey Sasaki, how're you doing?" Mr. Nomura called out. "You went to the City Hospital today, didn't you?" He stole a glance at Mr. Sasaki out of the corner of his eye.

"Yes, I'm going to the Red Cross Hospital all right, on Monday."

"Oh, the Red Cross Hospital, huh."

"She wanted to say goodbye to everyone," her father explained as he walked to Mr. Nomura's side. He continued in a low voice. "Looks like there's no way to avoid that hospital."

"Well, what matters is that Sadako get the best care possible."

"Right. We've told her that it's a lymph sickness. She'll find out sooner or later, but we're not saying anything about A-bomb disease."

"I understand."

The students, clad in their gym uniforms, crowded around Sadako, and spoke to her in surprised or encouraging tones.

After a few minutes, Mr. Sasaki broke in. "Sadako, we'd better get going."

"Hey, we'll come to see you," said one of the boys.

"Get well quick, okay?" As they reached out to grasp her hands, Sadako suddenly burst into tears.

"Now, what is this?" said Mr. Nomura, trying to make his voice sound rough. "Crying time?"

Sadako pursed her lips and opened her eyes wide, working to get control of herself. Her father touched her shoulder softly.

The two headed toward the exit, turning around frequently. The other Bamboos in their gym uniforms waved and yelled goodbye until they were out of sight, and shivered when a gray cloud passed over the schoolyard.

3

Remnants of Evil

I

On February 20, 1955, snow began falling at twilight and by late night over eight inches had piled up. It was a big snowfall for Hiroshima, and it toppled 800 meters of the roof built the spring before over the Hondori shopping arcade. When dawn broke on the twenty-first, the sun reflected brilliantly off the hills behind the city in Ushita.

That morning Sadako entered the Hiroshima Red Cross Hospital. She was temporarily assigned to a bed for emergency patients because the hospital was full. Dr. Joji Numata, deputy director of pediatrics and the doctor in charge of Sadako's case, gave her another careful examination. Dr. Numata was thirty-four years old at the time and had the gentle manner of many doctors who work mostly with children.

Dr. Numata checked Sadako's blood, and her parents' blood, and then asked if any of their relatives had blood diseases. He wanted to know all the details about what had happened to their family during the atomic bombing ten years ago. No matter what angle he explored, he found nothing to encourage any other explanations for Sadako's symptoms. It was clear that Sadako was being attacked by incurable, acute leukemia as a result of her exposure to atomic bomb radiation ten years earlier.

Leukemia. The disease was named by the German pathologist Rudolf Virchow in 1845. Virchow noticed that the blood of leukemia patients was chocolate colored. If it was allowed to settle in a test tube, an unusually thick layer of pinkish-white blood cells would form over the mass of red blood cells; hence the name "leukemia," the white blood disease.

To put it simply, leukemia is cancer of the blood. The organs that make blood, the bone marrow and lymph nodes, are attacked by a virulent disease that causes an uncontrolled production of leukocytes, which are white blood cells. Immature forms of leukocytes, either lymphoblasts or myeloblasts, which are normally found only inside the bone marrow and lymph tissue, begin to appear in the blood. These immature, often abnormal, leukocytes are called leukemic cells. Leukemia can be classified myelogenous, lymphatic, monocytic, or one of a number of other less common types, depending on the types of leukocytes that appear in the blood. Any of these types of leukemia can take acute or chronic forms.

When Sadako was admitted to the hospital, her blood contained 3,820,000 red blood cells and 37,400 white blood cells per cubic millimeter. A young girl ordinarily would have about 4,300,000 red and 6,700 white blood cells per cubic millimeter. Sadako's red blood cell count was somewhat lower than normal, and her white blood cell count was around five times higher than normal.

On top of that, Dr. Numata could see under a microscope that there were leukemic cells among her white blood cells. He could not tell if they were myelogenous or lymphatic, but it was obvious that Sadako was suffering from acute leukemia, the most fast-acting, most frightening form.

Generally speaking, the first symptoms of acute leukemia are weakness and increased fatigue. Leukemia patients are susceptible to bacterial diseases such as colds, and to bleeding from the nose and gums. Purple spots, signs of bleeding under the skin, can appear on any part of their bodies. The spleen, lymph nodes, and liver (organs that contain a lot of blood) swell, causing fevers that can be slight or quite high. The joints in the arms and legs become more and more painful. Finally the patient dies.

Chronic leukemia progresses slowly and patients can lead a normal life if they have proper care and supervision. Patients with acute leukemia usually do not last a year.

Several years later, in 1957, Dr. Numata would treat a two-year-old boy with acute leukemia who would grow up to marry, have healthy children, and lead a normal life. As of 1984, 30 percent of juvenile acute lymphatic leukemia patients (70 to 80 percent of all juvenile leukemia patients) could expect a complete cure. In the future that figure is expected to rise to more than 50 percent. In Sadako's time, however, acute leukemia led inescapably to death.

Even now we do not know what causes cancer, including leukemia, or understand how it develops. We know that certain viruses can cause leukemia in chickens and mice, and that certain chemicals can trigger it in humans. We know that radioactivity-induced leukemia followed the widespread use of x-rays in medicine, but we do not understand the cause in the same way that we know how certain bacteria cause certain diseases.

If the cause of a disease is obscure, the proper treatment will also be unclear. With other cancers, like those of the stomach or lungs, the diseased part can be surgically cut out of the body. Therapeutic radiation is another treatment. But the blood and blood-forming organs cannot be separated from the body, and radiation would only hasten the progress of the disease. The only treatment left is chemical agents, or drugs.

Even now, in the 1980s, there is still no wonder drug against cancer; back in the 1950s, sadly, no powerful treatment at all existed. Various medicines were being developed to regulate the production of white blood cells, and the progress of the disease could be slowed by blood transfusions from healthy donors—but both treatments only slowed the disease for a limited time. But even though the disease was considered incurable by medical science, Dr. Numata was far from resigned. The life of a young girl now in his care was being worn away by a demon, and he intended to pit all the strength he had against that demon.

Sadako was the first patient under his care who had contracted leukemia as a result of the atomic bomb. As a Hiroshima doctor, he had always assumed that such cases would come his way, but for the first to be an innocent twelve-year-old girl. . . . Because he was a pediatrician, all his patients were under fourteen, and some had died in spite of his efforts. But when he looked at this girl and thought about the event that had brought her here, he seethed inside. Why did this young life have to waste away because of a war that had been settled ten years ago?

For fifteen long years Japan had battled various countries. Ten years ago on August 15, it had all ended with Japan's surrender, barely nine days after Hiroshima was destroyed by an American bomb.

The war ended and peace returned to Japan, but for Hiroshima's doctors, August 6 was only the beginning of their battles. Ten years later they were still locked in struggle, trying to pry loose the talons the bomb had sunk deep into the survivors. It was a losing, heavy-hearted, tragic struggle. Now, youthful Dr. Numata had joined the ranks.

II

"Still," sighed Dr. Numata as he read the chart. Sasaki, Sadako. Born: January 7, 1943. Height: 139 centimeters. Weight: 31

kilograms. Indoor exposure to the A-bomb at Kusunokicho, near the Misasa Bridge. Distance from hypocenter: 1,620 meters. External injuries: none. Ill-effects following exposure: none apparent.

Sadako had spent the last ten years as a very healthy child. At her last routine checkup at the ABCC in June the year before, her red blood cell count had been 4,410,000 and her white 4,500, both within normal range. What on earth was this A-bomb disease? It was like a monster hiding low and breathing softly in her body for ten years, waiting. Then suddenly, just as she was stepping into the springtime of her life, it bared its fangs and turned violent.

The thermal radiation and blast alone made the atomic bomb that exploded 580 meters over Hiroshima at 8:16 A.M. on August 6, 1945 the most destructive weapon in history. The amount of radiation emitted with the blast put it beyond imagination.

The atom bomb uses the energy produced when neutrons bombard the nuclei of atoms at high speed, creating a chain reaction of atomic fission. This fission, or breaking up of atoms, releases enormous amounts of radiation. Four types of radiation are produced: alpha ray, beta ray, gamma ray, and neutron. Alpha and beta ray radiation are blocked by the atmosphere and do not reach the earth's surface, so it is believed that the radiation that affected human bodies at the time of the bombing was gamma ray and neutron radiation.

At ground zero in Hiroshima, a human body absorbed 10,300 rads of gamma radiation and 14,100 rads of neutron radiation. At one kilometer from the hypocenter the levels of absorption were 255 rads of gamma and 191 rads of neutron radiation. There is medical evidence that all human beings who receive more than 700 rads of gamma radiation (70 to 350 rads in the case of neutron radiation) die within a week or two, so anyone who was close to ground zero who somehow survived the effects of the heat and the blast would die of the radiation.

What's more, the radiation was not present only at the moment of the blast. The nuclear fission generated radioactive by-products. Some of the uranium, the basic raw material for the bomb, was spread around unfissioned, or unused, in its radioactive state. Other material in the area that absorbed neutron radiation at the time of the blast became radioisotopes, a form of atom that continues to emit alpha, beta, or gamma rays until it reaches a point of stability. Through a phenomenon called residual radiation, these products of the A-bomb continued to emit radiation for a long time.

The dirt and debris blasted into the air at the moment of explosion also absorbed radioactive rays before descending to earth. This came to be known as "radioactive fallout" or the "ashes of death."

Finally, from the mushroom cloud that formed after the explosion, a black rain began to fall in the north and western sections of the city. Later, chemical analyses found considerable residual radioactivity in these parts of the city. Great numbers of people who lived more than four kilometers from the city, but who were exposed to the black rain or "ashes of death," as well as people who came into the city after the bombing to help the victims, were exposed to residual radiation and died.

The initial radiation decreased in proportion to distance from the hypocenter, and buildings or other shelters offered a certain degree of protection. But no one in the entire area could avoid the radioactive raindrops or dust wafting through the air. Once these radioactive particles entered the human body, they retained their radioactivity for a long time; the victims of residual radiation were attacked from the inside out.

While some things were already known about the effects of radioactivity on the human body, this was the first time in history that so many people had absorbed so much so quickly. Immediately after the bombing, scientists began to speculate that radioactivity from an atomic explosion might have profound effects on the human body. The doctors of Hiroshima had no access to these speculations—but treating body after injured body, they gradually realized that this had been no ordinary bomb.

According to reports issued several years later, the symptoms of radiation sickness that showed up within two weeks included vomiting, hemorrhage spots, stomatitis (cold sores), dizziness, diarrhea, and disturbances in the blood-forming organs like the bone marrow. Within five weeks of the bombing came hair loss, anemia, and a decrease in the number of white blood cells. These symptoms appeared not only in survivors, regardless of burns and other external injuries, but also in those who had entered the city as rescuers during the first days after the bombing.

Most of those who began experiencing these symptoms within the first five weeks died before the year was out. As the flames subsided and peace gradually returned to Hiroshima, what thoughts did they have as they lay dying?

Both those who survived the initial stages of radiation sickness and those who escaped symptoms entirely until later suffered greatly over time as their bodies disintegrated from the late effects of the radiation. Even today, the damage done by radiation to human bodies is not totally understood; scientists think that radiation damages cells in the human body and exerts a particularly negative influence on lymphocytes, blood cells within the bone marrow, the intestines and testicles, the cellular tissue of the ovaries, bladder, esophagus, stomach, mouth, and pharynx, the outer layers of skin, the hair root, sebaceous glands, and eyeballs.

Thus, the illness generally referred to as "A-bomb disease" is not one distinct disease. Keloid, often (mistakenly) used as a synonym for A-bomb disease, is not a phenomenon connected only to burns from the atomic bombs. However, the keloids caused by A-bomb burns were abnormally large and not amenable to surgical treatment. Keloids began appearing in October

1945, two months after the bombing. Fortunately, they began to shrink after about three years; by 1949–50, the problem had largely resolved itself. Plastic surgery also became effective in managing these scars. Still, in 10 percent of all cases, keloids reappeared after every attempt at removal.

Cataracts began to appear among the survivors forty days after the bombing, in mid-September. A survey done by the department of ophthalmology at a local hospital from 1957 to 1961 revealed that among 128 survivors, 32 had cataracts.

Damage to the blood-forming organs is one of the late effects afflicting survivors even today. This damage leads to an abnormal decrease in red and white blood cells and blood platelets, causing a serious, malignant anemia. The postwar shortages of commodities and economic hardships undoubtedly dealt further blows to such patients.

Radiation not only harmed adults and children exposed to the bomb on that day, it mercilessly struck the lives of fetuses growing in their mothers' uteruses. Stillbirths and miscarriages occurred at eleven times the normal rates, and infant mortality up to five years was eight times higher than usual. Of those lucky enough to survive, many were born with microcephalia and other defects.

Hiroshima's Public Health Bureau released figures in 1960 showing that the rate of increase of cancer in Hiroshima was higher than the national average. However, cancer caused by radi- ation was an accepted medical fact even before the war, and cancer as a result of the bomb had been predicted. By 1955, ten years after the bombing, the death rate due to cancer among survivors had grown high. The rate was especially high among those exposed to 200 rads or more. Radiation exposure is connected to a wide variety of cancers, including leukemia, cancer of the thyroid, lung cancer, cancer of the esophagus, stomach cancer, bladder and other urinary tract cancers, and malignant lymph tumors.

Of these diseases, leukemia in particular began claiming victims only a year after the bombing; the yearly incidence increased dramatically after that, peaking at eighteen cases in 1951. For the next ten years, ten or so new cases would appear yearly. After 1965 it began to taper off, but even as late as 1972, nine new cases of leukemia were reported among A-bomb victims.

The national incidence of leukemia is two or three people of every 100,000, but among A-bomb survivors, especially those exposed closer than two kilometers from the hypocenter, it was 29.44 people per 100,000. Among those who entered the city within three days after the bombing, the rate was 7.75 per 100,000. Among those who entered within a week, the rate was 6.63 per 100,000. These figures (which do not include the Nagasaki A-bomb survivors) are obviously much higher than the national average. Studies have shown that even before *hibakusha* —nuclear weapon survivors—contract serious diseases, they are weaker and generally more susceptible than nonvictims. We are still waiting for the results of studies describing the effects of the A-bomb on mental health and heredity.

"A-bomb disease," an abbreviation of "Chronic Diseases of the Atomic Bomb," the term Dr. Masao Tsuzuki introduced in 1954, was a popular term used for several years after the bombing to describe a host of physical abnormalities.

And now, Sadako had been diagnosed as having an A-bomb disease that would probably only allow her another six months of life. But Sadako was full of energy. Her body might have been slowly decaying, but she had no fever or pain in her joints. A lymph node in her neck was swollen, but her liver and spleen were neither enlarged nor hemorrhaging. She had a good appetite. Evidently, the demon of leukemia had not penetrated into all her body systems yet.

Still, therapy had to begin right away; Dr. Numata started out with a blood transfusion. Pouring healthy blood into her veins was a temporary solution, but it would keep her blood corpuscles nearly normal for a while.

In those days, blood for transfusions was generally the responsibility of the patient, which meant the family had to work hard to obtain the blood. At first they could give their own blood, but if the patient required repeated transfusions, they would soon have to buy it from the public blood bank. No public health insurance or system of assistance for A-bomb survivors existed during Sadako's time. Her hospital expenses became another heavy burden on her father's shoulders.

Neither the doctor nor her parents told Sadako that she had leukemia or that her illness was in any way connected to the A-bomb. She must have been bewildered and alarmed when she had to be examined repeatedly at the ABCC and then enter the Red Cross Hospital. Still, she innocently believed that no matter how sick one was, getting a doctor's care in a hospital would fix the problem. The condition of her body gave her no clue that she faced death. For a growing twelve-year-old girl, full of promise, death did not seem real.

A short time after she entered the hospital, she wrote a letter to a friend in Miyoshi City:

Dear Michiko,

I am sorry for not writing you sooner.

I am fine and doing okay. I came into the Japan Red Cross Hospital on February 21. I'm not that bored because every day three or four of my classmates come to visit me.

I haven't been home even once since I was hospitalized, so I'm wondering if the neighborhood has changed. The other day, on February 20, the radio said the roof over the Hondori Arcade fell, so I went with Mom and everyone to see it. The roof was down, all right. No one was hurt but a couple of people had fainted. The roof fell at about 9:00 at night and they said that if it had fallen a little earlier some people would have been killed. After the snow a young woman was run over and killed by a car in front of the Chugoku Bank.

By the way, they put blood into my arm after I came to the hospital on February 28, and it really hurt. The doctor said if you don't hurt a little when you're sick you won't get well. I don't mind the pain if it means I can get well quick because I might get to go to your house during spring break. Please let me know if it's okay. If the doctor tells me to stay a little longer I might not get to go. Take care of yourself and please write. I'll be waiting.

Sincerely,
Sadako

III

Mr. Nomura spent some time wondering how to explain to the Bamboo class about Sadako. The family had told him that they had not spoken to her about leukemia or A-bomb disease, but surely she would figure it out eventually. At this point, rather than try to hide the truth from her classmates, he made up his mind that it was better to tell them exactly what was happening.

The morning Sadako entered the hospital Mr. Nomura stood on the platform and looked at the sixty-one faces lined up in rows. Only Sadako's chair stood empty and lonely, like the gap where a tooth has been pulled from the mouth.

"As you all know, Sasaki-san is in the Red Cross Hospital. Luckily, she's doing all right now, but she's got a pretty difficult disease. Sasaki-san was exposed to the A-bomb when she was little and that seems to be the cause."

The word "A-bomb" rode to every corner of the classroom on a wave of whispers.

"That's why Sada-chan kept going to the ABCC, isn't it?"

"A-bomb disease doesn't get well, does it?"

Voices murmured here and there.

Suddenly from the middle of the room in the seat next to Sadako's came the loud voice of Shinji Miyasako. "Mr. Nomura, is A-bomb disease catching?"

Shinji stared at Sadako's desk and chair with a strange look on his face. He had moved to Hiroshima when he was in the third grade.

Before Mr. Nomura could say "No," a sharp voice rang out from the back. "Idiot! If the A-bomb disease was catching, everyone in Hiroshima would have caught it a long time ago!"

"That's right. It's not contagious or anything. It's just whether you were here during the *pika* or not."

"No, it wasn't so much the ones who were here during the *pika*. It was the ones who came in afterward."

"My mom said the rain after the *pika* gave people A-bomb disease."

"That couldn't be. My older sister didn't get rained on, but she threw up blood two months after the bomb and died. It was from radiation, just like on Bikini. It's the ashes of death that kill you."

"It's like this. The people who lost their hair after the *pika* don't get A-bomb disease later. And the people who got burned or injured don't have to worry either. It's the ones who were healthy right along that are getting A-bomb disease nowadays."

Opinions about A-bomb disease—mostly popular rumors with little to support them—were popping up from every corner. But Mr. Nomura was surprised. About one-third of the class were survivors, but usually there was no way to tell them apart. They lived every day as if the bomb had no connection with them, but here they were brimming with information, scientifically based or not. They must have picked it up listening to family and grown-ups' conversations. But why had these children, some not yet twelve, been so quick to absorb it? Maybe they unconsciously felt threatened by the bomb.

When some of those who had not been in Hiroshima during the blast or soon after were innocent enough to ask if A-bomb disease was contagious, Mr. Nomura could not bring himself to scold them with, "You're ignorant," or "Show more consideration toward your *hibakusha* friends." The blame lay with parents who had neglected to tell their children the story of what happened to Hiroshima ten years ago on August 6.

"Poor Sadako-san."

Little more than a whisper, these words immediately wrapped the noisy class in silence. The coal-burning stove in the middle of the room hissed unusually loudly.

After awhile, sobbing was heard. Those who experienced the bomb, those who had lost family members, and those with no personal connection alike gave way to their sadness over Sadako, their classmate.

Mr. Nomura forced a tone of encouragement into his voice. "Listen everyone, we can't let Sadako face this long battle by herself. We've got to support her, cheer her, fight alongside her. The Bamboos are unified, right? So if one of us is suffering an illness, we all share the pain, don't we?"

"Can we go see her in the hospital?" asked Makiko Yamashige, raising her puffy eyes.

"Sure, just don't go tearing in there like a mob. Since we don't know when she'll be getting out, a few visitors at a time is enough. Let's take it slow so we can keep it up until she gets out."

"Let's get into groups and take turns."

"If we organize ourselves according to neighborhoods, it'll be easier to get together."

The suggestions kept coming.

And these were the Bamboos? Mr. Nomura thought back to that day in April last year when he first set foot in this classroom. Feuding constantly, each only looking out for himself or herself, they were a far cry from this group collaborating to support a sick classmate.

Soon the groups were formed; the first one prepared to head for the Red Cross Hospital right after school.

Mr. Nomura had a last comment to make about the visits. "One thing: no one has said anything about A-bomb disease to Sadako yet. So don't talk too much about her sickness."

Sixty-one serious faces nodded emphatically.

As if it had been waiting for her to come to the hospital, Sadako's illness took a turn for the worse. Her white blood cell count, which had been 37,400 at admission, increased with each test and was up to 65,400 two weeks later. That was ten times higher than normal. Her red blood cells were decreasing, down to 3,000,000.

Along with her regular blood transfusions, Dr. Numata now turned to chemical therapy. Methotrexate, just developed in America, was normally unavailable in Japan, but the Red Cross Hospital could obtain it free from the ABCC. This drug could control the number of white blood cells, but had no effect on the disease itself. And, because of the danger of side effects, it had to be used with great care.

Every day Sadako swallowed the small white tablets wrapped in red paper. She took one milligram of Methotrexate daily from March 14 to March 29, and the effect was dramatic. From 50,600 on the twenty-fifth, her white blood cell count was down to 16,600 on the twenty-ninth. Of course, this was still more than twice as high as the normal person's 6,700.

Around the twenty-fifth, the lymph node on her neck was obviously smaller than before, but in early April a new symptom appeared: spots of hemorrhaging beneath the skin on her chest.

In March Sadako moved from her emergency cot to a bed in a big room. Since the hospital did not separate the pediatric and obstetric wards, Sadako was assigned to a room full of adults. For someone whose body was undergoing such a radical change, Sadako appeared surprisingly strong. Except during quiet hours, she was out of bed. She often walked around the ward, befriending patients in other rooms.

Sadako and one other girl were the only children of school age. Since she had looked after her younger brother and sister at home, it was easy for her to be a kind older sister to the little children at the hospital as well. There were always two or three around her, and every day her classmates visited her after school. On the surface, it was not a gloomy life, but the brightness was limited to what was possible within the walls of a hospital.

Mrs. Sasaki closed the shop at nine o'clock every night and set off for the hospital after work to take care of her daughter. After the day's work and streetcar ride, Fujiko's exhaustion was obvious even to Sadako.

"It's late, why don't you go home?" Sadako urged. "Mitsue and Ei-chan must miss you." She had to shake her mother awake as she dozed next to the bed.

"You're right, I'll go home now," Mrs. Sasaki would answer, lifting herself heavily out of the chair and heading for the door. Walking down the dimly lit corridor together, they tried to mute the shuffling of their slippers. "Okay then. See you tomorrow night." Turning to face her daughter at the elevator, Mrs. Sasaki saw Sadako's thin shoulders inside the cardigan and eyes brimming with tears.

"If you're going to do that," she said, "mother won't be able to leave." Her arms reached out instinctively to wrap around her daughter.

The Sasaki family's finances were stretched to their limit. Not only was there Sadako's hospital fees, but the blood transfusions were expensive too. Some nurses were moved by the Sasaki's plight and donated their own blood, but that also had its limits.

Mr. Sasaki sold his wristwatch to a pawnbroker, bought blood at the public blood bank, and delivered it to the hospital.

IV

On Wednesday, March 16, the Bamboos had a goodbye party just before graduation. Groups that had taken care of cleanup duties together for a year now were preparing skits or songs. They carefully planned and rehearsed their parts for this occasion, the end of six years of schooling. The day's program was written on the blackboard; there were also pictures of the traditional New Year's decorations of pine and bamboo, a link to the class name.

After the opening words, the A-group began singing the song "Furusato"—Home Town.

> Chasing rabbits on the mountain side
> Fishing carp from streams. . . .

The children sang the old favorite with enthusiasm. This old wooden building that was Noboricho Elementary would later arouse warm feelings of home, just as the song did now. Perhaps because of such feelings, many of the songs the groups chose for that day looked to the past, having something to do with "that old place."

A little while after the activities had started, the arrival of Sadako Sasaki and her mother caused a small commotion. After her classmates told her about the day's party, Sadako had asked Dr. Numata for permission to come. "All right, go ahead," he had consented, after a moment's consideration.

Around March 16 her condition was fairly serious, yet he had boldly given permission for an outing. Since she had no fever, anemia, hemorrhaging at the joints, or other problems that normally accompany blood disorders, he decided that a little excursion would not harm her if she were careful.

Dr. Numata knew that Sadako had little time left. Why shouldn't she escape her bed and venture into the outside world while she still could? He gave permission for various outings, including overnights at home. His thoughtfulness must have been very heartening for Sadako.

The Bamboos were overjoyed by Sadako's appearance. Shouting their welcome, the girls surrounded her. Sadako was wearing the kimono with the bright cherry-blossom pattern under a short *haori* jacket with the same pattern, the one her mother and aunt had stayed up all night sewing just before she went into the hospital. When she was seated, the program resumed.

She especially enjoyed Toshio Yasui's funny long monolog from his cross-legged perch on the platform and Fumio Kumagai's enactment of "Big Ruckus on the Mountain."

When it was time for her to return to the hospital, she bowed and said politely, "Goodbye everyone."

Words of encouragement tumbled out here and there.

"Hurry and get well!"

"We'll be out to see you, okay?"

"I'm going to see Sadako to the door," Mr. Nomura announced, grabbing his trusty camera and standing up. It was spring but the air outside was cold.

"Sasaki, since you went to all the trouble to put that kimono on, I've got to get a picture of you." He had her stand in front of him. Through the viewfinder, the swellings on both sides of her neck were clearly visible.

"*Sensei* . . ." she began after the shutter clicked, staring at him fixedly. "What am I going to do about junior high school?"

"Junior high?"

"I thought I'd be out in time to start along with everyone but it looks like it's going to take a little longer."

"Oh, you don't have to worry about that. I'll do all the paperwork for you to get in." She smiled with relief. "Even if you don't get out in April, you can start in May or June or whenever. So you just get well, okay?"

"I will," she answered, nodding deeply. The bark of the cherry trees in the schoolyard was glossy in the afternoon sun. The few buds on the narrow twigs still looked hard.

After the class party, there was nothing to do except wait for graduation. The greenhouse that the entire sixth grade had worked on as a gift to the school was complete. They had raised it up themselves, hauling sand from the nearby Kyobashi River to mix into cement for the foundation. The 368 graduates had put together a book called *Omoide*, a book of memories, a collection of their poems and compositions. Every one of the sixty-two Bamboos had contributed something toward the collection, and so had their teacher. Mr. Nomura's contribution said:

> There is an old saying, "Time waits for no man." Shouldn't we treat each day as something precious? You who are pushing upward like bamboo sprouts every day are the adults of tomorrow. Live with great ambition and energy. Many dangers and difficulties await you, but I believe your strong will and unity will support you through all suffering. Be happy and healthy as you leave your old school this glorious spring and lead an honest life. I pray for your growth and prosperity.

Anyone who read those words and did not know the situation might find it an ordinary farewell message, but thoughts of Sadako had crowded into his head as he wrote it. She was one of the children preparing to set out alone into the future, but she would not continue to push up like a bamboo shoot. He could tell her nothing, except that she must make each day precious.

Tadaaki Ishimi had this to say about Sadako in his composition called "Kadode," or Threshhold:

> Soon we will be graduating. Even though we gave our teacher problems for a long time, I feel somehow sad that it's all ending. . . . Only one thing is left on the minds of our class: that Sasaki-san got A-bomb disease and is in the Red Cross Hospital. From our hearts we hope that she will get well as soon as possible and be her lively self again. . . .

Tadaaki had not wanted to neglect mentioning his ailing teammate in his composition, but when Mr. Nomura received it, he was put in a bind. A copy of these collected compositions would certainly find its way to Sadako, and then she would know she had A-bomb disease. Still, Mr. Nomura decided to risk including the piece as it was.

The students would always keep this collection. Picking it up as grown-ups, they would be reminded that a child in their own class had suffered A-bomb disease. Tadaaki's words would be the record to keep the memory alive.

As a matter of fact, Sadako's best friend Tomiko Yokota mentioned the A-bomb in her composition as well. She had been exposed to the A-bomb in Ushita and luckily escaped without a scratch. Her older brother had died, however, and Tomiko must have been thinking of him as well as of Sadako when she wrote her angry words about the bombing.

For Sadako Sasaki's contribution, Mr. Nomura selected a composition she had written about Field Day back when she was healthy.

Two days before graduation on March 23, the Bamboo class organized their Unity Club at the suggestion of their teacher. "All right, it's finally graduation time. You won't let everything you've worked for together just vanish now, will you? Why don't you form a group, so you can meet when you want to, even after graduation?"

Mr. Nomura had formed alumni clubs with graduating classes at his country school too. This would be his fifth Unity Club.

Whether or not the children would continue the club was up to them, but he wanted it at least to start. He would give them the name, but they would have to manage the club on their own. The children immediately agreed.

"*Sensei*, what kinds of things will this club do?"

"That's for you all to decide. Why don't you have a meeting right now to talk about that?"

The class representative walked up to the front and the meeting was called to order.

First, the Unity Club had to have a president. During their feuding days, this was the group that had scrambled over each other to become "big bosses" and "little bosses." There was no lack of candidates for the position of club leader.

Eventually, the younger of the Jigo twins, Nobuhiko, was elected over Yoshihiro Ooka, the leader of the Motomachi group. Obviously surprised, Nobuhiko walked self-consciously to the front, scratching his close-cropped head.

"Um . . . I'm not sure why, but I've been elected president of the Unity Club. Since I'm here, I'll do the best I can." He bobbed his head.

"Hey Nobu, you can't be so wild now that you're president," someone jeered.

"Idiot! Who's wild? I'm a good boy these days. If you want to see someone wild, look at Nao!" He wagged a finger at his look-alike elder brother.

"You'll be sorry for this," Naohiko snapped, glaring back.

"Now look, Mr. President," Mr. Nomura could not help interrupting. "If you're going to waste time like this, we won't get very far."

With Nobuhiko in control, the Unity Club set about laying down concrete plans. Voices piped up one after another. After graduation, the club would meet once a month at their old school. If any member got married, they would all contribute toward a gift. They even decided the amount of money they would offer the couple. (As a matter of fact, when Tomiko Yokota married over ten years later, they did present her with the agreed upon amount.)

Naturally, they took up the matter of Sadako Sasaki. Sadako would probably stay in the hospital. They agreed enthusiastically that the groups would continue to visit her.

On March 25, 1955, the sixty-two children of the Bamboo class left the nest, their Noboricho Elementary School.

4

Presentiment of Death

I

Shukkeien is the private garden built by Lord Asano who ruled over the area during the Edo period. Located along a wide curve of the Kyobashi River, the spacious garden contains a pond spanned in the middle by an arched stone bridge. Next to the pond is the Sentei Tea House. Local people have long been more familiar with "Asano's Sentei" than with the name of the garden. The majestic old trees that framed the pond for centuries were destroyed either by the blast or by the fires of the atomic bomb; now a handful of young trees cast their scrubby reflections in the water. But people still come out in all seasons to enjoy the restful atmosphere of "Asano's Sentei."

Noboricho Junior High School was located just to the east of Shukkeien. With 2,500 students and 65 teachers, it was the second largest junior high school in the city. The twelve classes of the seventh grade that entered in April 1955 were forced to attend school in two shifts until June.

Masako Yamaguchi, one of those seventh graders, lived near a streetcar stop in Nagarekawa. The raging fires of the atomic bomb had burned her family's large mansion to the ground, leaving no trace of it amid the ashes. The family now included Masako, her two older sisters, her mother who worked as a kindergarten teacher, and her grandfather, a veteran. They lived in a rickety barrack thrown up on a corner of their land.

Masako had played with Sadako since they were small. Together they had eaten the figs that grew in her yard. But Masako sometimes envied Sadako, who still had both parents and a sister and even brothers. After Japan's surrender, Masako's father, a graduate of the Imperial University in Tokyo, was recruited as an interpreter for the military tribunal in Yokohama. Just after the atomic bombing he returned to Hiroshima as part of a survey team and roamed through the devastation every day. He died suddenly in late September, presumably killed by residual radiation from his experience on the survey team.

Because her mother had a job, Masako was under the strict rule of her grandfather. He had her doing housework whenever she was not in school. Stunned when she heard of Sadako's sickness, she felt her old jealousy slip away. Masako had lost not only her father but grandmother and aunt to A-bomb disease. "Now Sada-chan is sick with the disease that killed my father. Lively Sada-chan, suffering just like my father and grandmother." Even as sadness came over her, she felt a new closeness to Sadako.

Between her many chores, she was always looking for a chance to drop in at the hospital. On April 6 she visited Sadako after the entrance ceremony at the junior high school. As she was leaving the house, her eye was caught by blooming primroses in the corner of the yard. Sadako had helped her plant them the previous fall. She dug up the fullest blooms, placed them in a pot, and took them to the hospital.

Sadako looked better than she had during spring break. Noticing her friend's new navy blue uniform, she said, "Masa-chan, today was the school entrance ceremony, wasn't it? How's junior high? Have the classes been assigned?"

"Uh-huh. I'm in the third class, out of twelve. Lots of kids from Hakushima Elementary and Ushita Elementary came to Noboricho, that's why there're so many classes."

After thinking for a minute, Sadako murmured, "I wonder which class I'm in."

"I'm sorry, I should have found out. The names are all posted in the hall. I'll find out tomorrow and call you."

"Don't worry about it, I'll find out soon. How are the Bamboos doing?" she asked, changing the subject.

"The ones at Noboricho seem okay. Oh, Kumagai-kun was absent."

"Why, is he sick?"

"Uh, he had surgery for tympanitis. He'll be out for a month. Oh, here's this," she added, placing the pot on the bedside table. "Remember the primroses we planted last fall? They're blooming now."

Sadako's eyes grew round. "They're blooming? So soon?" She leaned over, almost touching her face to the pretty, light pink petals, and gazed at them for a long time. "Yeah, because it's already spring, isn't it?"

When she entered the hospital on February 21, there had been snow on the ground. Now spring was in its peak. "I have to hurry and get well too," she added, as if to herself.

"You seem better than you did last time."

"Uh-huh, because my white blood cells are way down."

Masako started. Did Sadako know what she had? She changed the subject casually. " 'Otena's Tower' isn't very interesting these days. 'Benikujaku' was much better." The popular children's serial was regularly broadcast on NHK radio Monday through Friday at 6:30 P.M.

"Oh, that's about Hokkaido, isn't it? I used to listen to it when I was at home. You know, I haven't heard 'This Week's Star' or 'The Children's Music Contest' since forever. Sometimes the person next door lets me listen to Hibari-chan's songs on her radio." Sadako loved Hibari Misora. She was always humming the singer's tunes and hanging her photographs and magazine cut-outs on the wall.

The next day at school, Masako pored over the class lists posted on the wall. She found Sadako's name under class six.

Now junior high students, the Bamboo group still managed to visit Mr. Nomura frequently at school and at home. The Unity Club had promised to meet monthly, but that was not the only reason. Junior high school was cold and impersonal to the new seventh-graders; getting through every day was a strain. There were new subjects like English and manual and home arts. And now every subject was taught by a different teacher. At after-school clubs, they felt threatened by the older students. On top of that, now they had to wear uniforms. The boys wore stiff, stand-up collars, and the girls, navy blue jumpers with jackets.

Going through their routines with hunched shoulders, they waited for Sundays. Some of them would find each other and wind their footsteps over to Yoshijima-cho. There they would find their old playground, unchanged. No older students to handle with care, no fearsome teachers to make them tremble. No one to jeer at boys and girls for spending time together. They would lose themselves in play, sixth-graders again. Afterward, they would drop in at the Red Cross Hospital on the way home.

Yoshijima was just across the river from Sendamachi, where the hospital was. Visiting Sadako after a hard day's play somehow made the children feel guilty. They felt sorry for their sick friend having to hear about all the fun over at the old airfield or down by the sea.

Once, Nobuhiko Jigo, Shinichiro Hayashi, and Kimiya

Haguma stopped in at the hospital after visiting Mr. Nomura and collecting shellfish on the beach. When they entered Sadako's room, she was sitting on her bed, making a decorative paper ball. She had always been nimble-fingered.

"Hey, how ya doin'?" Nobuhiko greeted her in his usual loud voice.

Sadako nodded with a smile and hopped off the bed, suggesting that they go up to the roof. These days, Sadako always took her classmates up to the roof. She wanted to keep the bouncy junior high students away from the other patients in the large room. Her friends never thought about the reason for the trips to the roof.

They stepped out onto the roof of the old concrete building, where the usual lines of clothes were hanging to dry. "You went digging for shellfish, didn't you?" asked Sadako, peering into the cloth bag hanging from Nobuhiko's hand. The heavy-looking clams were blowing bubbles.

"Yeah. Because the tide was just right today. I got the most."

"Ummm. They look good."

At that, Nobuhiko whipped the bag behind his back. "Don't get any ideas, I'm taking these home."

Chuckling, she turned to face Shinichiro. "Did you join the baseball club?" The quiet boy laughed shyly.

"Oh, he's in the baseball club all right. What a joke! He hasn't done anything but chase balls so far."

"The Noboricho team is just right for Shin-chan. It'll be second rate forever, just like the Carp." Kimiya could not resist adding his insults too.

At that, Shinichiro faced Kimiya to defend Hiroshima's team. "Oh, yeah? This year's Carp are different. Now they've got Hirayama and Zenimura. Plus, Hasegawa's looking good this season."

The Hiroshima Carp had been struggling to survive ever since they were established as the city's professional baseball team in 1950. Even though—or perhaps because—they stayed at the bottom of the central league, the people in Hiroshima, especially the young boys, loved them dearly. In April that year, when two Japanese-Americans named Tomoo Hirayama and Kenshiro Zenimura joined the team, 100,000 people crowded into the city's main streets to welcome them.

"Hayashi-kun, I thought you'd join the art club since you're so good at drawing."

"Well, I, um, wasn't sure what to do but I, uh, ended up in the baseball club," he stammered while she gazed at him.

"Oh, I just remembered. My mother said to tell you to be sure to come over next time you spend the night at home," threw in Kimiya. Their families lived next door and were friends, but ever since Sadako had ended up in his class, Kimiya tried not to play with her too much. The Bamboos were unusual in that boys and girls got along well, but because they were close neighbors, Kimiya somehow felt shy and had to start keeping Sadako at a distance.

"Thanks. I'll be over for sure," she replied and looked around as if she had just noticed something. Twilight was setting in.

"Shouldn't you be going home?" The sun was starting to shimmer on mountain tops in far-off Hatsukaichi. Sadako's face, which had become quite pale, was dyed pink by the setting rays.

"I guess so," said Nobuhiko, acting as spokesman. "Well, we'll be back. Get well quick, okay?" They started over to the elevator while Sadako watched, grasping the railing.

"Goodbye!" She waved at the boys.

"Get well fast!"

As soon as they were out of the hospital, Shinichiro turned to Nobuhiko. "Monkey was crying, wasn't she?"

"She was?"

"Yeah, she was."

Kimiya turned to Nobuhiko accusingly. "Probably because you wouldn't share your clams with her. Why didn't you give her a few?"

"Oh. I guess I should have." Nobuhiko's voice was unusually meek.

Unity Club members visited Sadako religiously, and not only those at Noboricho. Yoshie Kato, Hiroko Nejime, and Kazuko Hikiji, who went to private girls' schools, would come to the hospital with the others.

Around this time, club members put out a little money and bought Sadako a pair of male and female *kokeshi* dolls. They were very ordinary carved wooden figures, but Sadako was overjoyed. She kept them with another doll given to her in the hospital beside her bed until the end.

The "Kokeshi Club," which was formed in later years, took its name from the dolls that Sadako loved.

Even Ken Hosokawa, who went to a private boys' school, visited Sadako now and then. Ken's house in Saka-cho in the eastern part of the city was far from any of his former classmates' homes, but his Shudo Junior High was near the hospital, so he occasionally dropped in on his way home.

Since Ken's home was far from the city's center, he had not suffered any direct harm from the bomb. But his older sisters had commuted to a girls' school in the city at that time. He dimly remembered their coming home that day, blackened with dirt. Luckily they were still healthy, but Ken knew the fear of the bomb.

He had never had much to do with Sadako, except for playing together a few times at Mr. Nomura's. Now he was a visitor at her bedside, but that did not necessarily give them anything to talk about. A boy at a boys-only school and a girl stuck in a hospital world had little in common. After "Get well fast," what was left? Still, Ken found his way to her bedside time and time again, and not only because of the Unity Club vow. Maybe it was the air clinging to her of the sixth grade class that drew him. He had never even visited Mr. Nomura much—but Sadako Sasaki ended up his closest friend among the Bamboos.

On May 31, the Sasaki family sold their house of eight years in Teppocho and moved to a barrack on the bus line in Motomachi. The move was a last-ditch effort to manage the bills of Sadako's hospitalization as well as to repay the old debt. The move from the city's main street to a dirty row of barracks near the Aioi Bridge revealed the state of the Sasakis' finances.

And, while Sadako's white blood cell level was stable, her internal organs, particularly her spleen, began to swell. Sometimes her temperature rose to around 100 degrees. The disease was slowly ravaging the young girl's body.

II

Kiyo Okura entered Hiroshima Red Cross Hospital in December 1954. She was in her second year at Kokutaiji Junior High. Kiyo had a tubercular infiltration of the lungs that would require lengthy treatment. The fourteen-year-old became the oldest patient in the pediatric ward.

Since she had become ill, her life had been reduced to a miserable fight against disease. She was an only child whose father had died soon after she was born. Mother and daughter had never had it easy, but a twosome had certain kinds of freedom. Then, with the onset of her illness, their world crumbled at a stroke. According to the doctor, Kiyo would be in the hospital for at least six months and would then have to recuperate at home another six months. That meant missing a year of school. The fourteen-year-old girl was sure that repeating a year in school would throw her entire life off course.

At first she kept her spirits up by thinking, "I got sick and now I just have to get well." But as the monotonous hospital life wore on, she alternated between impatience and despair. Her friends who had visited her so frequently when she was first admitted began to stay away after the start of the new school year. They had been eighth-graders together, but the others had moved on and she had not. Perhaps they felt she was no longer one of them. Someone her age in the hospital might have been a comfort, but unfortunately there were only preschoolers in the pediatrics ward.

No, actually there was one girl about Kiyo's age. A girl named Sadako Sasaki had come to the hospital toward the end of February. Kiyo had heard about her through the whispered conversations of the nurses and the adults in her room. Kiyo knew the girl had a very serious disease called leukemia that had to do with the atomic bomb, and that she would not get well.

A strange fact about hospitals is that, before you know it, you know more about other people's conditions than they know themselves. When Kiyo first heard the rumor about Sadako, she was quite shocked. The girl had A-bomb disease. She stared at Sadako from a distance and sympathized with her.

However, despite the sad rumor going around about her, Sadako was amazingly bright and cheerful. Within a week of entering the hospital she had befriended the other children on the ward and had become a favorite of the women in her room. Could the girl really have a serious illness? Watching Sadako run up and down in the hall and up to the roof, Kiyo felt somehow tricked.

Kiyo herself, since entering the hospital, had done nothing but curse her disease. She had snapped her shell shut like a clam. Perhaps growing up alone with her mother had made her ill at ease with others. She rarely made much contact with the women in her room, and the little children were, to be frank, a bother. She was willing to play with only a very few. Naturally, the other patients and nurses came to walk a wide circle around her. At least, that's how it seemed to Kiyo.

Sadako was in every way her opposite. "Sada-chan! Sada-chan!" The adults and children always calling to her sounded so familiar and warm. Wherever she went, two or three little children trailed behind. When Kiyo saw Sadako having her hair braided by an adult patient in another room, the cozy scene gave her a little stab of jealousy.

For all these reasons, when the two girls were transferred in May to the same room near the elevator, Kiyo felt no great welcome.

"Kiyo-san, aren't you lucky? Since Sada-chan is around your age, you'll have someone to talk to." Kiyo made herself nod dutifully at the nurse's words.

Sadako too was a little apprehensive about living with this prickly older girl. Still, she gave her a friendly smile, bobbed her head, and said, "This will be nice."

Their room was on the second floor of a wicket-shaped building. There were other patient rooms on either side, and the door on the south end led to the hall. The only window was on the north. Outside they could see the rows of windows of the surgery and internal medicine wing, and below, the neglected garden in between. Their beds were placed perpendicular to the window. Their north-facing, shabby old room was a dreary place, but Sadako did not mind. She covered the wall next to her bed with photographs of Hibari Misora, and stood her *kokeshi* dolls on the side table, and in no time she had made it her castle.

Kiyo pointed to the dolls and said, "They're cute."

Sadako's eyes lit up. "The kids from my sixth-grade class went together to buy them for me," she explained happily. "I like Hibari-chan. Who do you like?" she went on sociably.

"I'm not interested in popular music. I like reading books."

"Oh." Sadako gazed at her, impressed. "I read stories from

Shojo or *Shojo Club* sometimes. Oh, and I borrow copies of *Jogakusei no Tomo* from my friends." She stumbled slightly over the names of the girls' magazines—*Young Girls, Young Girls' Club, Girl Students' Companion*—as if she were trying them out.

Kiyo spoke with affected dignity. "Now that you're in junior high, you should start reading literature by famous authors, like Soseki Natsume and Ogai Mori." Sadako listened, her eyes widening with surprised respect. Kiyo softened a little toward the younger girl. Maybe they would get along after all.

Not that she would go out of her way to open up to Sadako. The little children would be following her around all the time, and then there were her friendships with adults; Sadako had friends not only in pediatrics and obstetrics but in the internal medicine and surgery wards too.

One clear day, as a prank, a patient from the surgery ward used a mirror to flash light around the girls' room. In a second, Sadako leapt from her bed and dashed out of the room, grabbing her hand mirror. She hurried to a room that got direct sunlight and asked the patients to let her in. Running to the window with her mirror, she gave the man a taste of his own medicine. It was this kind of quickness that had earned her her nickname of "Monkey" in school.

Kiyo envied her liveliness. She restrained the part of her that wanted to run about too, and instead spoke sharply to her. "Sada-chan, would you mind being a little quieter? I'm trying to read."

"Oh, sorry," Sadako would mumble in shame, burrowing soundlessly under her covers.

These days when Sadako's friends came, she took them straight up to the roof out of regard for Kiyo. The seventh-graders always came in threes and fours and managed to be noisy even standing together in a clump. Her friends did not stay long. In thirty minutes at the most, Sadako rode the elevator back down to their floor. Only when she walked back in the door after one of these visits did Sadako have a lonely air about her. Her friends had progressed to a new life in junior high school, while she alone was trapped in this white hospital room. Even Kiyo could imagine how Sadako must feel.

There were times when jealousy got the better of her. Sadako was spending the night at home once or twice a month, and her family came to the hospital whenever they could find the time. Her mother in particular visited faithfully, and often spent the night. Most people would have seen the plumpish woman and the small-framed girl cradling each other as they slept as the picture of a loving parent-child relationship, but they made Kiyo feel uncomfortable.

"Look at them," she thought, wanting to cluck her tongue. "And Sadako in junior high. How can they?" Perhaps because she had been a working woman since before the war, Kiyo's reserved mother would never think of lying with her daughter. Kiyo herself certainly had outgrown the need for that kind of relationship. Or maybe she really did want to cuddle up to her mother, but . . .

Going into June, Sadako's condition worsened. For a while the lymph nodes in her neck had shrunk, but now they were swollen again. When the doctor examined her spleen he found a stiff lump about the width of two fingers. Continuous transfusions were keeping her white blood cell count between 10,000 and 20,000, but this was still more than twice the normal level.

Around that time a five-year-old girl in the same ward died. Like Sadako, she had had acute leukemia. She had been a fair-skinned little girl, still just a baby. Naturally, Sadako and Kiyo had known her well.

The night she died they decided they wanted to say goodbye to her. Her body was laid out in the hospital mortuary. They usually avoided this frightening room of the dead even during the day, but that night they entered without a trace of fear. The girl looked like she was sleeping, in the small coffin lying in front of a simple altar. Kiyo and Sadako lit sticks of incense and pressed their palms together prayerfully for a long time.

Outside was the continuous drone of *tsuyu*, the rainy season. Their vigil finished, they were returning through the dim corridor connecting the wards when Sadako, walking behind Kiyo, suddenly stopped.

"I wonder if I'm going to die like that."

At that soft mutter, Kiyo turned around in astonishment. Standing in the middle of the hall, Sadako was staring out into the dark, wet garden.

"Don't be stupid!" Kiyo's hands reached instinctively for Sadako's shoulders. This was the first time she had ever touched her. Her fingertips felt Sadako's boniness through the thin cotton robe. How could the bouncing Sadako she knew every day be this thin and feeble?

"*Nei-chan*—Big Sister . . ." Sadako pressed her head against Kiyo's chest and began to cry.

"This girl knows what she has. She knows and she's trying desperately to bear up under it." Suddenly, Kiyo saw Sadako's everyday behavior completely differently. Her constant liveliness, the childlike relationship with her mother, it was all part of her battle against the fear of approaching death. Kiyo cried, "Sada-chan," and her heart went out to the girl in her arms. Within Kiyo's embrace, Sadako wept as if she would never stop.

Meeting Kiyo was Sadako's sole comfort during the last months of her life. Ever understanding of Mitsue and Eiji at home, and helpful to the little children at the hospital, Sadako found in this new relationship her life's only opportunity to bury her face and cry into the chest of an older sister.

After this night, Sadako and Kiyo opened up to each other without reserve.

III

As if they had just been waiting for a new month to begin, Sadako's white blood cells began increasing again in July. The number of platelets in her blood dropped and her gums began to bleed. The hardened part of her spleen was now more than three fingers wide, and her lymph nodes swelled.

On July 18 her white blood cells were recorded at 108,400, by far the worst yet. Dr. Numata began the Methotrexate treatment again. Blood cells and liver notwithstanding, Sadako was amazingly energetic. During this month she had no fever and continued to eat well, as she had since entering the hospital. Somehow, the transfusions were keeping her going.

The rainy season ended and Hiroshima moved into one hot day after another. The Unity Club members, who had never slackened throughout rainy season, now gradually slowed the pace of their visits. Junior high school was becoming a comfortable world, and the pressure of club activities and school work mounted.

The 1955 Noboricho Junior High summer schedule was:

> July 24: School closing ceremony
> July 25–August 3: Special summer study
> July 28–August 3: Baseball training camp
> July 25–31: Gymnastics training camp
> August 4–7: String orchestra training camp
> August 4–9: Girls' volleyball camp
> August 8–10: Art training camp

And so on.

For all grades, the summer study program filled the days until the beginning of August, while the training camps lasted anywhere from three days to a week. In elementary school, summer vacation had meant free time, but junior high was different.

In mid-July, some high school girls in Nagoya sent a box to

the Red Cross Hospital "For the A-bomb Patients." The box contained one-thousand multicolored paper cranes folded out of cellophane paper and strung together. Most of them were distributed to the A-bomb patients in the internal ward, but one of the strings found its way to Sadako through a nurse.

Paper cranes were not new to the girls—Kiyo's mother had made a large crane for each of them and hung them from the ceiling of their room—but when high school girls sent one thousand of them in strings, Sadako was very excited.

"Aren't they pretty?" she exclaimed, turning to Kiyo. "Let's make some ourselves."

"Okay," Kiyo agreed, fascinated by the string of little cranes brightening Sadako's bedside. Neither knew that these presents had been sent especially to A-bomb patients, and Kiyo was a little jealous that only Sadako had received a string. Later, someone told them why the cranes had been sent, but Sadako seemed neither shocked nor distressed.

The two of them threw themselves into folding cranes. They soon discovered that regular-sized cranes were awkward to fold lying in bed. After trying a variety of sizes, they found that a five-by-five centimeter piece of paper was big enough to handle and small enough not to tire the hands.

The first thing was to get the paper. They started out with the paper their medicine came in, and wrappings from presents, candy and caramels. They cut big sheets into strips five centimeters wide, and then cut those to make squares. They soon used up all the papers around them, and began to walk around the ward together asking for pretty pieces of paper.

Neither disliked this kind of painstaking work. Sadako had always liked making paper balls and braiding sandals with paper strings. Laboring over the precise folds of tiny cranes, they distracted themselves from the abundance of time.

Whenever they accumulated fifty, they strung them together.

There were heating pipes under the ceiling on opposite sides of the room. They ran a string between these pipes. Whenever they had a new string of fifty, they hung it from the string between the pipes. New cranes appeared constantly.

One day, as Sadako began a new crane by folding a square piece into a precise triangle, she suddenly said, "They say you'll get well if you fold a thousand. I wonder if it's true."

"Hmm."

"You'll get well from your sickness, won't you? Whether you fold a thousand cranes or not."

Kiyo glanced swiftly at Sadako on her bed. Lying on her back, she was completely engrossed in the crane she held in front of her face. Her exposed white arms seemed almost transparent. By that time Kiyo's condition was improving daily. She would almost certainly leave the hospital by the end of summer. But Sadako . . .

Kiyo casually changed the topic of conversation. "Sada-chan, how many have you folded?"

"Uh . . . 472 . . . no, now it's 473."

"473! I've only got 380. Okay, I'm going to catch up."

When she tired of folding cranes, Sadako wrote letters or read books. Under Kiyo's influence, the girl who had never picked up anything but girls' magazines was now reading literature. She read Ogai Mori's short novel *Gan*—Wild Geese. Following Kiyo's advice, she began exchanging letters with a girl her age whose name she found in the "pen pal" section of a girls' magazine.

July 30, 1955

Dear Taguchi-san,

I am feeling much better lately. I am also very happy to have a good friend like you. Thank you for your get-well card.

The thing I like best is music. My favorite flower is the rose. My favorite star is Hibari Misora. My favorite foods are pears and grapes, etc.

I am a seventh-grader at Noboricho Junior High. I was born on January 7, 1943.

Please tell me the name of your school, your birthday, your favorite hobby, flower, star, and foods. Please tell me in detail.

My address is: Motomachi Hondori, Hiroshima City.

I'll let you know when I get out of the hospital. Goodbye.

Sincerely,
Sadako Sasaki

Sadako wrote the first draft of letters or cards in her notebook and then copied them over. She wrote summer greeting cards to every person in the Bamboo class.

To Sadanori Fujimoto,

This is my summer greeting card to you. How are you doing, Fujimoto-kun? The summer study program must be hard work. Be careful what you eat and take care of yourself in this hot weather.

I am going to get well and be back in school soon.

Goodbye

When she tired of writing letters and reading, she headed for the hospital garden or the rooftop.

Once in a while the two girls would go up to the roof at night to gaze at the stars or enjoy fireworks from the Sumiyoshi Shrine. The night after the young girl with leukemia died, the rainclouds lifted, leaving a clear night sky full of blinking stars. They stood on the roof for hours, their heads craned upward, searching the sky. Surely the soul of the dead girl had transformed into a brilliant star. The lovely night sky seemed to invite such sentimental thoughts. After that, the two of them often went up on the roof to gaze at the stars.

Such a universe, spreading outward without limit. How small human beings were in comparison.

Sadako had feared her death many times. The disease that was wracking her body came from radiation and could never be cured, she did not need to be told that. But death was so vague to a twelve-year-old. Dying is frightening. And sad. But what happens after you die? Even when fear had clutched her heart, it was no worse than a scary dream, nothing with any real power over her.

However, seeing the peaceful face of the dead five-year-old girl had made death real. Always so weak before, the image of death now fastened itself to her mind. Once your white blood cell count exceeds 100,000, you die. The rumor going around the internal ward had reached Sadako's ears recently. Of course, it had no basis in fact; her white blood cell count on July 18 was over 100,000. Still, the rumor must have made her feel keenly the closeness of her own death.

After Sadako's death, it was discovered that she had been secretly recording and hiding under her bed the data from the blood tests conducted on her regularly since her admission. After each test, she had penciled on a piece of rough newsprint the counts of both red and white blood cells and the amount of hemoglobin. How this twelve-year-old was able to obtain test data withheld from patients remains a mystery.

Sadako roamed the hospital with such freedom that she was even allowed to answer the phone in the nurses' station. She must have peeked at her chart lying on the desk, and she could have asked the nurse what the figures crowded onto it meant. The nurse could have answered offhandedly that those represented numbers of blood cells. But asking permission to record them for herself would have been going too far; Sadako would have waited for the nurse to leave the room before she copied them.

What was she thinking? Sadako alone in the nurses' station, bent intently over the task of copying the counts of her own blood cells onto that paper.

5

A Crane That Can't Fly

I

The time of year when Hiroshima remembers "that day" was coming around again. It was not a day the Sasaki family was likely to forget either.

On August 6, 1945, Hiroshima was just beginning another hot summer's day. The city was built on a delta at the mouth of the Ota River, which flows from its source in the Chugoku Mountain Range. Under Lord Asano during the Edo period, Hiroshima was a flourishing castle town, a fiefdom capable of yielding 430,000 *koku*, or over two million bushels of rice. The Meiji period saw Hiroshima develop into the political, economic, and cultural center of the Chugoku region. The Chugoku Regional Imperial Military Headquarters and other military facilities were established in the vicinity of Hiroshima Castle, and the city's Port Ujina became the base for invasions into China and Korea.

There are conflicting opinions about the number of people in

Hiroshima on that day. There were civilians. There were draftees stationed there as well as professional soldiers working at the military facilities, and their families. There were also thousands of Koreans forcibly brought to work at factories like Mitsubishi Heavy Industries. Mobilized citizens were working to demolish buildings in the city to make firebreaks for protection against American air raids. Students mobilized from city schools were working in factories. All told, there must have been around 350,000 people in the city at 8:15 on the morning of August 6.

But this number refers only to those who were in the city at the moment of the blast. It does not include those who entered the city soon afterward, or those on the outskirts, who were exposed to the radioactive rain. Even today, no one has come up with a reliable count of all the secondary victims, but various data indicate that the number is somewhere around 90,000. In other words, around 440,000 people were directly exposed to the harmful effects of that single explosion.

There is also considerable debate about the number of deaths. On August 20, 1945 the Hiroshima Prefectural Governor's Report set the number of dead and missing at 42,550; as information about the bombing has accumulated over time, that number has continued to grow. When the mayor delivered his "Peace Declaration" at the Peace Memorial Ceremony in 1951, he proclaimed that some 200,000 precious lives had been lost to the bomb. At the present time, the most reliable figures set the number of dead between August 6 and the end of November at 130,000. If so, of every four people exposed to the bomb, one died.

At 1:40 A.M. on August 6 (Japan time), a B-29 called the Enola Gay and three accompanying observation planes took off from an American military airport located on Tinian, one of the Mariana Islands in the Pacific Ocean. One broke formation to stand by on Iwo Jima Island; the rest continued toward Japan.

Passing over Iwo Jima Island at 6:41 A.M., they received weather reports on Hiroshima, Kokura, and Nagasaki cities from three preceding observation planes. Based on these reports, they chose Hiroshima as the target. Until this moment, they could have headed for any of the three cities, depending on weather conditions.

The weather observation plane flying over Hiroshima had caused the Chugoku Regional Military Headquarters to sound an air raid alert at 7:09 A.M.; but the plane soon disappeared and the all-clear was given. No one in the entire city could possibly have imagined the scene from hell that would envelop them forty-five minutes later.

Because of two air raid alerts that had been sounded the night before, some citizens had spent the night in air raid shelters. But after they heard the third all-clear signal, the people of Hiroshima gradually moved into their morning bustle. Actually, nightly air raid warnings had become such a common occurrence that people were not particularly alarmed by the presence of "B-sans," as the Japanese had nicknamed the B-29 bombers.

Ironically, until "that day," Hiroshima had never experienced a real air attack. Except for two incidents when small explosives were dropped on March 18 and 19 by ship-based fighters and a B-29, there had not been a single fatality. One after another Tokyo, Osaka, and even other cities in the same prefecture such as Kure and Fukuyama had been reduced by carpet bombing to burnt fields. Miraculously, the devastating war had left Hiroshima without a scratch.

"Hiroshima is definitely safe," her optimistic citizens told each other.

At 7:31, after the all-clear sounded, the city was alive with morning energy. The demolition teams moved into action at 8:00, the time most businesses and factories began their operations. Charcoal-burning vehicles sputtered their way across the

Aioi Bridge, while at Zakobacho, girl students wearing head bands and work trousers began clearing away the debris of wooden buildings that had been taken down.

In the homes, breadwinners had been seen off for the day, and housewives were clearing the rice bowls from their scanty wartime breakfasts off the dining tables.

According to the Hiroshima District Meteorological Observatory, at 8:00 A.M. on August 6, 1945, Hiroshima's weather was overcast with high clouds. Cloud coverage was "10," with three types of clouds recorded; cirrus, cirrostratus, and cumulus. All the clouds were so high that the people on the ground saw a typical, slightly white, beautiful summer sky.

With 80° Fahrenheit (26.7° Centigrade) and 80 percent humidity at eight o'clock, the morning heat was moving in. The offshore night wind changed to a light sea breeze shortly after eight. The sun bore down with increasing intensity.

Just before 8:15, at the inner city Hiroshima Central Broadcasting Station (NHK) in Nagarekawa, a warning was transmitted to the information room. The announcer began to relay it into the microphone. "8:13 A.M. The Chugoku Regional Military Headquarters reports three large enemy warplanes advancing over Saijo. . . ."

The remainder of his message was lost in the flash and roaring blast.

Sadako Sasaki, in her dining room, must have experienced this flash and deafening roar as well. At the time, the Sasakis' home and barbershop were close together at 1-chome Kusunokicho, in the northwest part of the city. Since Mr. Sasaki was an army medical orderly stationed at Miyoshi City in the northern part of the prefecture, Sadako's mother and her Aunt Chizuko ran the shop. Grandmother Sasaki, who was seventy-six, mother Fujiko, then twenty-six, Sadako's brother Masahiro, then four, and Sadako, thirty-one months old, lived in the house, while

Sadako's Aunt Chizuko, thirty-five, and her daughter Fujie stayed at the shop.

At 8:15 A.M. the Sasakis were sitting down to a late breakfast as the three B-29s invaded the sky above the city from the east; one had just dropped three parachutes bearing observing and recording equipment. Then, at 8:15 and 30 seconds, the Enola Gay, from 9,600 meters above the earth, dropped its bomb.

Three meters long, seventy-one centimeters in diameter, and weighing four tons, the torpedo-shaped uranium-235 atom bomb fell from the sky for 50 seconds until it exploded about 580 meters above the Shima Hospital at 19 Saiku-machi (now 1-5-24 Otemachi).

Within one-one-millionth of a second, the explosion was a superhot one million degrees centigrade. At one-ten-thousandth of a second a fireball of 300,000 degrees had formed and expanded to a diameter of thirty meters. Two-tenths of a second later the ball was 400 meters wide and a blazing 7,700 degrees; the enormous fiery sphere enveloped the city sky for ten seconds. For comparison, the sun's surface temperature is 6,000 degrees centigrade.

These astronomically high temperatures melted and blistered roof tiles on houses within one kilometer of the explosion. It would be necessary to burn a roof tile with an acetylene torch for several seconds to achieve this effect.

Almost without exception, people within 3.5 kilometers who were caught outside suffered burns from the thermal rays wherever their skin was exposed to the explosion. Those closest to the center, of course, died instantly, regardless of clothing.

Houses more than three kilometers away burst spontaneously into flame. Within three kilometers, clothes that had been hung dripping on the line seconds earlier smoldered and caught fire.

At the same time, a powerful blast stormed the city. It has been estimated that near ground zero the gale traveled faster than

600 meters a second for about one second. Ordinary explosions only last about five or six thousandths of a second.

The buildings within a two-kilometer diameter all collapsed except for those that had been reinforced against earthquakes. All wooden buildings within four kilometers collapsed. Roofs were blown off some buildings within six kilometers.

Violent blast, raging heat, and radiation. The damage of an atomic bomb is the composite effect of these three factors. Persons near ground zero received 10,300 rads of gamma rays and 14,100 rads of neutron rays. Five hundred meters away the dosage was 2,709 rads of gamma rays and 3,015 rads of neutron rays.

Today we know that 700 rems is a fatal dose. Three hundred rems is fatal in 50 percent of cases. The International Commission on Radiological Protection recommends that the yearly permissible dose of radiation for persons in the vicinity of nuclear power plants be set at 0.5 rems. In Japan the target figure is 0.005 rems. "Rem" is a unit used to talk about dose of affecting radiation, but we can think of it as meaning the amount of damage to living things. The affecting dose of one rad of gamma rays is one rem; one rad of neutron radiation is 2 to 10 rems.

As explained before, the radiation of the atomic bomb was not limited to that emitted at the moment of explosion. Radiation was also present in the "ashes of death" and the "black rain." After the explosion, the mushroom cloud towered over the city at 17,000 meters and extended over an area of five kilometers. It slowly disintegrated and drifted northwest over the city as far as Kake-cho in the mountains, spreading "black rain" over an oblong area twenty-nine kilometers long and fifteen kilometers wide.

Pouring profusely in some areas and sprinkling barely enough to wet the ground in others, the rain was everywhere the oily, sticky substance its name suggests. Of course, at the time no one guessed that it was full of radioactive particles. It was generally thought that the American military was spreading combustible oil from the air.

No one imagined that a bomb beyond description had been dropped on the city. Ninety percent of the people assumed that a regular bomb had been dropped right on them.

II

The Sasaki family, located 1.6 kilometers from ground zero, believed that too. Although the explosion blew the roof off the wooden two-story house and crumbled the walls and pillars in a heap, fortunately their house was not smashed to bits. When Mrs. Sasaki collected herself, she called out to her children. Four-year-old Masahiro crawled out, crying, from beneath the low dining table. Its thin legs had held under the pressure of the beam and tatami mats that had fallen on it, and it had protected the small boy. But he did have a head wound that was oozing blood. Searching the kitchen, Fujiko found Sadako. The two-year-old was crying, sitting on a tangerine box that had fallen from upstairs, as though someone had perched her there. The blast had flung her onto the box, but there was not a scratch on her body.

Fujiko herself had no serious wound, but there was a great gash on Grandmother Sasaki's arm. She hurriedly tended to her arm and Masahiro's head, grabbed the children's hands, and went outside. Their street ran between the Misasa Bridge and Yokogawa and was fairly wide—but it had completely disappeared. The telephone poles were down and the street was covered with columns and roofs of totally destroyed houses. It had become a vast heap of rubbish.

A hazy mixture of smoke and dark clouds obscured the sky and turned day to twilight. Human silhouettes, mostly wounded, moved about in a daze on top of the debris.

Fujiko stood dumbfounded. Before long, the smell of burning wood began wafting through the air. Flames licked from openings in the collapsed houses. As if in a dream, her feet began moving toward the river. Along the way many voices cried for help from the fallen houses over which she scrambled, but she could not stop her feet.

When they finally reached the foot of the Misasa Bridge, Grandmother Sasaki suddenly stopped. "There's something I need to go back for. You go ahead." Before Fujiko could stop her, the elder Mrs. Sasaki had disappeared back into the expanding curtain of black smoke. It was the last time anyone in the Sasaki family saw her.

Although she was worried about her mother-in-law, Fujiko Sasaki had to take care of the two small children. Reluctantly, she headed down to the riverbank.

The west bank of the Ota River running along Kusunokicho 1- and 2-chome had long been called the "*Unjoba*," the Landing. During the Edo period, logs had been floated down that far, then hauled up onto the land. Until this morning, an army hospital and ammunition storehouse for field artillery had stood on the opposite bank. Hiroshima castle's five-story tower had risen out of the thick greenery beyond. But the magnificent Rijo Castle and its surrounding forest were gone. Red and black flames engulfed the entire horizon beyond the opposite river bank. By now, Fujiko understood that the attack had not centered on her house; she understood vaguely that a destructive force of unimaginable power had been unleashed on them.

The riverbank between the Misasa Bridge and the railroad bridge upstream was crowded with people seeking safety. High tide had peaked at 8:05 A.M. and the water had begun its slow drift out to sea. The shallow Hiroshima rivers allowed sea water to climb a fair distance upstream when the tide came in. Subsiding enough to create tidelands during low tide, the water at high tide stood more than two meters deep in some places.

Turning back toward home, Fujiko saw that the area between the Kusunoki and Misasa neighborhoods was a mass of whirling flames. Now even the houses immediately behind them were igniting.

When they got upstream of the railroad bridge, the flames pushed them down from the stone wall onto the sand.

"Sasaki-san! Come over here and get in!" Luckily, a neighbor called them over to a little river boat. The old, abandoned row-boat began leaking under the pressure of the more than ten people who clambered into it. Naturally, it was impossible to paddle upstream against the tide. Dropping anchor midstream, they could only try to protect themselves from the flames lashing out from both banks.

Both the Hakushima and Misasa riverbanks were a blazing sea of fire. From time to time a fierce crackling arose as the flames consumed something new, spewing fiery sparks and forming a whirlwind that blew across the water. Red hot tin sheets from roofs cut through the air and disappeared into a cloud of white steam in the water.

"You in the boat, come over here!" Voices pleaded to them for help from the bank, but no one moved. If they had approached the bank the boat would have been engulfed in the flames licking onto the water, or it would have sunk under the weight of the crowds scrambling aboard.

After awhile, the pleading voices faded. Some had drowned, many had been roasted by flame and heat. Fujiko and the other occupants silently continued to bail water out of the boat. A little after 9:00 A.M., they heard the drone of a B-29 in the dark sky. Somewhat later came a patter as drops of a black, oily, liquid splattered them.

"The B-sans are covering us with oil so we'll burn better," someone murmured.

More like heavy oil than water, the foul-smelling substance stuck to them. Sadako's and Masahiro's white shirts were soon stained black. The shirts were later washed many times, but the stains never disappeared.

The rain just drizzled where they were, but in Kogo in the western part of the city a heavy downpour lasted thirty minutes. In Koi and other places, the "black rain" was followed by regular rain, which put out the forest fires.

Gradually, as the tide continued to ebb, the white sandbar surfaced here and there. At 1:00 P.M., with both banks still ablaze, Fujiko Sasaki decided to get off the boat. The receding waters brought into view people rolling about on the riverbed, too injured to move, some half-incinerated. The scene on the Hakushima bank was even more hideous. Lashed by the flames until they had tumbled and fallen, hundreds of black bodies lay on each other like stacked lumber.

Stepping through the bodies, the three of them began walking upstream on the white sand. When they got to Oshiba, an area with more tilled fields, the flames were gradually dying out. They climbed the river bank, coming up near Oshiba park. Cherry trees had toppled, broken at the base—yesterday's green, rustling leaves were brownish-red. Beyond the park, the huge 500-year-old camphor tree in Shinjo Shrine and the straw-thatched farmer's house beneath it whirled up in red flames. There was no room to walk in the park. It was packed solid with exhausted inner-city refugees crouching on the ground.

A virtually naked woman was standing, her hair frizzed as if from a permanent. At first glance, tatters of clothing seemed to be hanging from her ankles and wrists, but a closer look showed that it was her own peeled skin. Thermal rays of more than 6,000 degrees and a wind traveling 600 meters a second had peeled off the entire top layer of her skin.

"I'm cold. . . . I'm cold. . . ."

The burned people were all complaining of the cold. Though clogged by black smoke and dust, the midsummer afternoon was far from cold; yet they wanted to be covered with clothing or blankets.

An old woman was pulling something like a sash hand over hand into her kimono. Near her a man who could not help noticing said, "Ma'am, forget the sash, throw it away."

She angrily replied, "What! These are my intestines!" A closer look showed that her intestines were indeed spilling out of a great gash in her abdomen. The old woman was desperately trying to pack her own organs back inside her body.

"Water . . . water . . . ," called voices here and there.

"No, you can't have water. Listen, you can't give water to burn victims!" shouted a man dressed in the uniform of the citizens' defense reserve, walking among the people. At the time it was believed that drinking water caused burn victims to weaken and die. The man himself was injured, walking about with a piece of a rafter embedded in his back. "If I pull it out now, I'll bleed to death. So I'm going to put up with it, even though it's a little heavy," he bragged, as he tended briskly to the other wounded.

It was a nightmare, but people did not feel the horror. From the second the bomb exploded, the capacity to feel terror or sadness or revulsion was lost; people simply gazed blankly at the scenes in front of their eyes.

"All those with injuries gather at Oshiba National Elementary School! There's an emergency first-aid station there now!" a young woman clad in work trousers shouted through the megaphone.

"Where is it?"

"It's just up this way, so please walk." Those who were able staggered to their feet and headed in the direction she indicated. But most remained crouched where they were. Stretchers and carts for carrying the severely wounded had long since run out.

Fujiko Sasaki had started looking for her sister-in-law Chizuko a little while earlier. Because Chizuko lived with her daughter Fujie in the shop, she would seek refuge here if she were alive. Come to think of it, Fujie was a mobilized student, and would have gone somewhere in the inner city today.

She was also worried about her mother-in-law. If Grandmother Sasaki had somehow survived after disappearing into the flames, she would eventually end up here.

That afternoon, team after team of rescue workers came rushing in from the Kabe area. Some came in on their own, worried about relatives in the city. Some neighborhood associations even organized groups and came in on trucks.

Around nightfall, a coal-burning truck stopped near the park. "Anyone who wants to go to Miyoshi, get aboard!" Already a number of injured people were lying on the truck bed. Snapped to her feet like metal to a magnet, Fujiko grabbed her children's hands and ran to the truck.

"Excuse me, I'd like to go to Kamikawatachi. Will you take us?"

"Sure. Hurry and get on."

As if it had just been waiting for them, the truck set off. Coal-burning trucks had been developed during the war because of the gas shortage. An incinerator in the front of the bed partially burned coal and coke; gas from the incomplete combustion was sent into the cylinders to explode. It produced nothing like the horsepower of a gasoline engine.

Everyone on the truck bed was given some crackers, a kind of small, rectangular hardtack with two little holes baked into the surface. People called them "*kata pan*" or hard bread. Not having eaten since morning, Fujiko and the children crammed the *kata pan* into their mouths.

As night enveloped the truck in darkness, the sky over Hiroshima glowed an eerie red. "They say Hiroshima has been completely wiped out," muttered a man whose face was half-covered by a triangular bandage.

An estimated 130,000 people were dead. An estimated 5,187 houses were totally destroyed; 18,350 houses were partially destroyed. Everything within a radius of two kilometers was completely consumed by fire. Ninety percent of the buildings within three kilometers were consumed by fire and/or in ruins. Hiroshima had become a city of death.

But the terror did not end on this day. Wounded, barely escaping with their lives, the survivors were to live the rest of their days dreading the after-effects of the radiation.

III

They arrived at Fujiko's old home in Kamikawatachi at midnight on the sixth of August. Leaving her little children there, Fujiko went back to Hiroshima the following morning.

She met Chizuko at Oshiba Park, where she and the children had been the day before. Chizuko had been able to escape the collapsed barbershop and wind her way through the flames to the park. She had no word of her daughter Fujie, who had set out that morning for Dohashi-cho to demolish buildings. The two women also had to look for Grandmother Sasaki.

Together, they walked along the bank of the Ota river. When they reached the foot of the Misasa Bridge, they stopped in their tracks. In front of them stretched a burnt plain. Nothing remained standing to interrupt their view of the entire expanse. A reddish-black desert stretched from Kusunokicho, where their house and shop had been, to Teramachi, Tokaichi, and Dohashi, with Eba Mountain eerily close in the background.

Across the river from Hakushima to Motomachi and Hatchobori in the distance, black smoke still wafted above the ruins. The shape of a building that could have been Fukuya Department Store occasionally appeared through the smoky haze.

The two walked on in silence. The ground still smoldered enough to burn the skin. Hundreds of bodies floated in the river. Soldiers were fishing them out onto the bank with hooked poles, where they lay, grotesquely bloated. Here and there were piles of black-burned bodies. The bare-chested soldiers doused them with heavy oil and burned them.

Neither Fujiko nor Chizuko felt horror at these scenes, or revulsion from the stench. Carefully, they studied the black bodies of those about to be cremated, and inspected the scanty possessions removed from those already cremated. Nearby, other survivors similarly concerned about loved ones wandered about peering into the faces of corpses.

The morning clouds gradually burned off, leaving an uninterrupted blue sky by noon. The sun beat mercilessly on the steadily hotter earth.

Gathering information from people they met, Fujiko and Chizuko decided to make a round of the emergency first-aid stations scattered around the edge of the city. If their family members were alive, they were probably being cared for at one of those stations. They forced their feet to carry them from Mitaki to Koi, Furuta, Kusatsu, Inokuchi, and finally to Itsukaichi in Saeki County.

Emergency first-aid stations had been set up at national elementary schools and in the main buildings of temples and shrines. Any blankets or straw mats that could be gathered were spread out to accommodate the masses of severely wounded. Medicine and medical supplies had been exhausted the day before. Physicians were powerless to help their patients. They could only paint burns with zinc oil and cover wounds with mercurochrome.

The people brought to the stations were dying, one after the next. As soon as each dead body was carried out, another critically wounded person was carried in to take its place. Outside the windows where the wounded lay, members of local young men's clubs cremated the corpses.

A teacher who searched the shelters for his students during those days, himself injured on the back, wrote the following poems:

> Laid on the floor on nothing but a shabby straw mat, reed screens barely hold back the outside air.
>
> Losing even the sense to recoil from dead bodies, I look for traces of my students—nothing else.
>
> Pleading for water, a patient lying in the aid station extends an arm alive with maggots.
>
> Finding a student's name in a list of the dead, my heart is eased, forgetting grief.

Those who could confirm the deaths of their loved ones were the lucky ones. Many had no idea even where their loved ones had died. The unmourned dead were buried in the scorched earth.

Uncovering no news of Grandmother Sasaki or Fujie, the two women turned back in failure toward Miyoshi.

It was Shigeo Sasaki who finally traced Fujie and his mother. As a medical orderly stationed at Miyoshi Junior High, he entered Hiroshima with an emergency relief team to transport the wounded. Because the emergency stations around the city were bursting beyond capacity, the injured had to be transported to hospitals outside the city, or even beyond to hospitals in Yamaguchi Prefecture.

On the ninth of August he finally got some time to head for the site of the Sasaki home at Kusunokicho. There, a neighbor he ran into had news of both Grandmother Sasaki and Fujie.

His mother had burned to death in a fire prevention water tank near the house and had already been cremated. "Why did you go back to the house for some trifle at a time like that? Why didn't you escape with Fujiko and the others?" Reproaching her, Shigeo gathered her scanty bones into a sack. "Who else would scold his mother as he collected her bones?" he thought to himself.

In the same way he learned of Fujie. "Your niece, she's in some temple in Kabe. She's burned bad. She told them she was the daughter of the Sasakis who have a barbershop in Kusunokicho."

Shigeo finally identified the temple in Kabe. When Fujiko and Chizuko rushed there, fifteen-year-old Fujie was already bones, leaving behind nothing but her cherished cloth purse. In all, the Sasaki family lost twelve people to the atomic bomb.

Fujiko had somehow escaped and Shigeo had not entered the city until the day after, but their exposure brought sudden changes to their bodies. Their one comfort was that their two small children seemed to be growing up in good health, with no abnormalities. And now, cruelly, ten years later that one comfort was disappearing. The ghost of "that day" had taken possession of Sadako, their healthiest child.

On August 6, 1955, the Sasaki family, including Sadako for the first time in a long while, ate breakfast together. She had been allowed to leave the hospital overnight.

Ever since the Memorial Cenotaph had been completed, the Sasaki family had gone every year to pay their respects. The monument stood in the oasis of green called Peace Memorial Park between the Hon and Motoyasu Rivers. After the saddle-shaped Cenotaph had been built in 1952, the annual official Peace Memorial Ceremony was held in front of it.

They had moved to Motomachi in May; their new home was

only a ten-minute walk from Peace Memorial Park. "It'll be eight o'clock soon. Sadako, do you feel up to the walk?" She jumped up cheerfully in response to her father's question. Sadako had survived a second dangerous period in mid-July, and now her white blood cells had declined again.

"Well then, shall we go?" Mr. Sasaki surveyed his family. How many months had it been since the whole family had gone anywhere together? Last-born Eiji leapt about happily.

"Ei-chan, we're not going there for fun, you know." Mitsue scolded her brother. "We're going to honor the people who died because of the *pika*." Mitsue had bravely assumed his care since Sadako had gone into the hospital.

They were off to pay their respects, taking along Sadako, who claimed to be fine but was in fact quite ill. Leaving their house and following the river, they came to the T-shaped Aioi Bridge standing at the junction of the Hon and Motoyasu Rivers.

On "that day" the atomic blast had buckled the bridge and toppled the entire railing off the side. A streetcar, wrenched off its rail, flung near the foot of the bridge, and burned down to the metal frame, had lain just where the Sasakis now walked. People said that the skeletons inside were lying in neat rows.

On the other side of the street stood the remains of the Industrial Promotion Hall, the bare framework of its dome and collapsed outer walls starkly outlined against the summer sky. At some point the name "A-bomb Dome" had stuck to the ruins that were now overtaken by summer grass and surrounded by barrack-type shacks. Some of the shack dwellers were selling heat-blistered roof tiles, warped bottles, and postcards as souvenirs. One of the shopowners would, on request, display the keloid scars on his bare back. Accused by others of "selling the *pika*," he retorted, "Is that so? Well then, what have you all been doing for the suffering *hibakusha*?" Four years ago, together with a group of volunteers, this man had formed the "A-bomb Victims

Rehabilitation Society," which struggled to find ways to help *hibakusha*. This was probably the first instance of *hibakusha* organizing themselves into a group.

As the Sasakis approached the dome, sirens throughout the city sounded in unison. It was 8:15, the time of the atomic explosion. From the opposite side of the bank, the bell pealed in a loud "Gong." The six Sasakis spontaneously lowered their heads and clasped their hands, each heart overflowing with its own emotion.

When the one-minute silent prayer ended, a bloody taste welled in Sadako's mouth. She furtively blotted it with her handkerchief, which was soon drenched red. "Sada-nei-chan's bleeding!" shouted sharp-eyed Eiji.

"What happened?" asked her mother, bending toward her face.

"It's nothing, just some blood coming out from between my teeth." Even as she made herself smile, fresh blood oozed from her mouth.

"We better get back to the hospital." They abandoned their visit and caught a streetcar for Ujina near the bridge.

Bleeding from the gums is one symptom of leukemia. As the white blood cells increase in number, the platelets that control clotting decrease in inverse proportion.

That this should happen on this day at this time . . . Sadako's parents felt a strange alarm.

Sadako faced out the window so that the strangers on the streetcar could not see her mouth. She sang softly,

> In the place where our city was destroyed
> Where we buried the ashes of the ones that we loved
> There the green grass grows and the white waving weeds.
> Deadly harvest of two atom bombs.
> Then brothers and sisters you must watch
> And take care that a third atom bomb never comes.

In 1954, nine years after the bombing, this song had appeared as part of the national "Signature-Collecting Campaign against A- and H-Bombs," which sought to ban nuclear weapons. Sekiji Asada had written the lyrics to "Genbaku Yurusumaji" (Never Again the A-Bomb) and Koji Kinoshita had composed the melody. (The English lyrics were written by Ewan MacCall.) The song was becoming well known in Hiroshima, and Kiyo had taught it to Sadako just two weeks before.

The wheels of the streetcar made the familiar clang as they made the wide right turn at the Kamiyacho intersection.

IV

Nineteen fifty-five was a memorable year for Hiroshima. The city-sponsored ceremony on August 6 broke its attendance record with more than 50,000 people. The "First World Conference against A- and H-bombs," which started on the sixth and lasted three days, made history by conveying the voices of *hibakusha* to the world for the first time. Over fifty delegates from eleven countries attended the conference, along with 5,000 Japanese delegates. Representatives of countries holding nuclear weapons sat down together with representatives of countries that did not, to seek ways of abolishing nuclear weapons.

On the second day of the conference, *hibakusha* faced the delegates of each nation and related their personal stories. Some delegates, like those from China, visited *hibakusha* in their homes or in institutions.

On the third day, the "World Conference against A- and H-bomb Hiroshima Appeal" went out to the world. Of course, the drive to abolish nuclear weapons was not something that had been born overnight. "That day" had firmly planted a terror and hatred of nuclear weapons in the citizens of Hiroshima and Nagasaki. Seven months after the bombing, in March of 1946, the

Chugoku Bunka, a publication of Hiroshima's literati, had published a special edition of articles that discussed and indicted the atomic bomb. Sadako Kurihara's "Umashimen Kana" (Let's Help Them Bear) appeared in this publication. In 1947, Shinoe Shoda's "Sange" (Falling Flowers), which rendered her personal experience of the A-bombing into *tanka* (31-syllable poems), was published illegally, in spite of the prohibition during the U.S. occupation against any publications dealing with the A-bomb damage.

Voices crying for the abolition of nuclear weapons rose also from the country that had dropped the A-bombs, and in 1948, a "No More Hiroshimas" movement became active in the United States. However, in the international atmosphere of U.S.–Soviet confrontation after the Second World War, these voices were completely ignored. In July of 1946, the United States tested its first atomic bomb since the end of the war in the Pacific Ocean, and in August of 1949, Russia conducted its first test.

The outbreak of the Korean War in June 1950 brought on a powerful oppression of the peace movement in Japan. Even the city-sponsored annual Peace Memorial Ceremony was canceled that year. The British nuclear weapon test in October of 1952, followed by U.S. and Soviet hydrogen bomb tests, demonstrated that the new world situation offered no escape anywhere from the threat of nuclear weapons.

In March of 1954, the crew of the Japanese fishing boat *Daigo Fukuryu Maru* became victims of radioactive fallout from an American nuclear test. When this news hit the only country that had experienced nuclear devastation, new waves of shock and rage spread through the nation. Although not reported at the time, it was later discovered that the crew members of the *Daigo Fukuryu Maru* were not the only victims of the test; many residents of Micronesia suffered after-effects.

This incident moved many people who had been unconcerned

about nuclear weapons to join the wave of protest. New interest was focused on Hiroshima and Nagasaki, the two cities that had fallen victim to the bombs. The groundswell of interest in peace bore fruit in the establishment of the "World Conference against A- and H-bombs."

Sadako Sasaki wrote a letter to her pen pal:

> Dear Takeda-san,
>
> Hello, it's good to hear that you are doing well. I am very well, too. I came into the hospital on February 21 and am getting better day by day. It's nice and cool in the hospital. Let's have fun when we see each other for the first time, okay? I also am a victim of the A-bomb and am in the hospital because of it. I went to pay my respects on August 6 and sang "Genbaku Yurusumaji." Even since I came back to the hospital, I'm still singing it in my bed. . . .

She evidently sent this to a child hospitalized like herself for A-bomb disease. Sadako wrote that she was getting better, but in fact she was worsening daily. Along with her spleen and lymph nodes, her liver was now swelling. Since August, her gums had been bleeding occasionally. Her white blood cell count had been temporarily depressed by Methotrexate, but mushroomed again after August 11.

Kikue Itadani, Sadako's teammate in the relay, visited her in mid-August. In the month since she had last seen her, Sadako had lost an astonishing amount of weight. On top of that, purple spots had appeared on her ankles.

"What's wrong?"

"Nothing," answered Sadako, slipping her feet under the futon. By that time Sadako was no longer taking her guests up to the roof. She spent the greater part of her day in bed.

Around this time she and Kiyo both finished their thousand paper cranes. Each had a big tassel of cranes at her bedside. At first they had been worried whether they could reach their goal, but once started, the project carried the girls along. Now that they were done, the girls wondered what to do with themselves.

"Sada-chan, are you going to stop now?"

Considering for a moment, Sadako shook her head. "No, I'm still sick. I'm going to fold them till I get well."

"Okay, then I will, too." Each girl started another thousand.

By this time Kiyo was almost well. Waiting for the day of her release, she began throwing her medicine into the trash behind the nurse's back and stopped taking her temperature properly. She was no longer a serious patient.

Sadako, on the other hand, had always faithfully followed all instructions from the doctors and nurses. She took her medicine carefully. When Kiyo tossed her medicine and tricked the nurse about her temperature, Sadako watched at first in great surprise. In time, she came to imitate Kiyo.

Every morning, when a nurse appeared to ask their temperatures, Kiyo would invent an answer. "Oh, mine was 97.7°."

At that, Sadako would invent her temperature as well. "Mine was 97.7, too." Sometimes she would throw her medicine away. This was no malicious revolt against the hospital, but a game to while away the monotonous hours.

Naturally, the doctor found out. Kiyo was scolded mildly. The severity of Sadako's scolding surprised Kiyo, who was lying next to her. "Sadako's illness must be much worse than she and all of us think," thought Kiyo.

At the end of August, Kiyo's nine-month stay in the hospital was over.

"I'm glad for you, Onei-chan," said Sadako, glowing as if she were the one getting out.

"You get well too. I'll come and see you when things settle down," said Kiyo. The plan was for her to recuperate at her relatives' home in Gion.

"Um-hum." said Sadako. "When I get well I'll go and see you.

It's a promise, okay?" She gazed at Kiyo with moist eyes.

Gathering her cranes from the walls, Kiyo left with her mother. The nurses and small children went to see her off at the entrance. "We have much to thank you for," said Kiyo's mother, bowing to the nurses. Behind the children, Sadako leaned against a pillar in the entrance.

Kiyo raised the cranes in her arm in farewell, and said "I promise I'll come see you." Sadako waved her hand slightly in response.

It was the last time Kiyo would see Sadako.

After Kiyo's departure in August, there were signs that the leukemia had entered the final stages.

On August 24 the Hiroshima Peace Memorial Museum was opened in the Peace Memorial Park; on September 19, the "Japan Council against A- and H-bombs" (*Gensuikyo*) convened for the first time. The demand for a hospital for A-bomb victims had intensified a year earlier, leading finally to a concrete proposal. The A-bomb hospital was to be built adjoining the Hiroshima Red Cross Hospital. For Sadako, these events came too late.

V

The midday sun felt like summer, but morning and evening breezes were noticeably cooler now. A little boy had moved into Kiyo's bed. The spoiled child spent most of his time crying.

Sadako no longer had the mental or physical energy for looking after the little children. And she was lonely after the only friend she could lean on—her big sister—left the hospital. She stayed in bed all day, folding cranes.

She reduced the size of her paper from five-centimeter squares to two. The new size made tiny wings, which she painstakingly creased with the aid of a toothpick. She continued to fold as if possessed.

"You'd better not push yourself too hard," her father warned, but Sadako laughed off his advice.

On September 28, her white blood cell count was recorded as 67,000, and her platelet number had reached a new low. Purple spots of subcutaneous bleeding were appearing around her chest, the lymph nodes under her arms and on her groin were swelling, and her internal organs were noticeably enlarged.

On October 1, typhoon number 22 whirled through Hiroshima and left autumn in its wake. The morning low on the thirteenth was 43.8° Fahrenheit. Eleven degrees cooler than average, it was early November weather.

Sadako's temperature, which had been hovering at around 98.6, climbed to almost 104 that morning. She lost what little appetite had remained, and the purple spots spread from her chest to her back, and even up to her face.

The girl who had been a runner speeding over the ground at this time last year now looked miserably thin. She was suffering with a temperature of more than 104 degrees, but her consciousness was uncommonly clear and she responded distinctly to Dr. Numata's questions.

On the sixteenth, she had a severe pain in her left knee. Her face was grotesquely swollen.

"Does it hurt badly?"

Knitting her brows, she nodded.

"Why don't I give you a shot for the pain?" Dr. Numata said, signaling to the nurse.

"Doctor, don't pain killers slow down the healing process?" she asked as she inhaled deeply.

"Yes. If you can stand it, it's better to stay away from the shots. But too much suffering is bad for your body too."

"I can stand it," Sadako answered decidedly. "I don't mind."

From the doctor's viewpoint, Sadako's condition could not be worse. He decided to use a new medicine, an adrenocortical hormone medicine called cortisone. Common today, in Sadako's time cortisone was impossible to obtain in Japan. The hospital got it from the ABCC, as they did Methotrexate. Cortisone shots were Dr. Numata's last resort.

Sadako was now too weak to walk on her own. The pain intensified daily, spreading from her joints to her lower limbs to her entire body. She gritted her teeth and bore it.

The only diversion from pain left to her was making paper cranes. Her trembling fingertips folded one after another as she lay in bed.

By now she had made another 500 cranes, which added up to a total of around 1,500. Of course, she did not achieve this all by herself. She was aided by members of the Unity Club who still visited her sporadically. Those friends did not perceive the gravity of her condition.

She lacked even the strength to string the cranes and hang them from the ceiling, as she had done before. The pile of little cranes grew in an empty candy box beside her bed.

After the twentieth of October, headache was added to high temperature and acute pain in her lower torso. She endured this also. And she endured going to the toilet. Using a bed pan would have been an intolerable indignity to a twelve-year-old girl. Of course, she could not go on her own strength. Her mother, who stayed at her side after the sharp decline in her condition, carried her on her back. Sadako was as light as a small child.

After October 23, the intensity of the pain coursing through her body made it hard for Sadako to sleep through the night; on the twenty-fourth the joints of her hands and feet turned purple, resembling dead tissue. That night, unable to sleep, Sadako watched morning come.

On October 25, just after 8:00 A.M., the phone rang in the Sasaki home at Motomachi. It was Fujiko Sasaki, calling from the hospital.

"Shigeo . . . Sadako . . . The doctor says we should get every-one here." Her urgent tone told Mr. Sasaki that the day had come. Watching Sadako these last days, he had thought he was pre-pared; but listening to his wife's voice, his heart began pounding.

"All right. I'll get the children." Then he realized that both Masahiro and Mitsue had already gone to school. Quickly, he called Noboricho Junior High and left a message for Masahiro to pick up Mitsue and go to the hospital. Then he set out himself with Eiji.

When he reached Sadako's room, she was still conscious. "Sadako . . ." His daughter barely opened her eyes. Without thinking, he cried out to Dr. Numata, who was holding her arm and steadily reading her pulse. "Doctor, please do something! A shot! Give her a shot!"

In a low voice the doctor gave an order to the nurse, who injected serum into an arm covered with purplish spots. Again Sadako closed her eyes.

Mr. Sasaki spoke desperately to his daughter. "Is there any-thing you want to eat?" If he remained silent, fear would burst his heart.

"Don't worry. I don't want anything," she answered hoarsely.

"You didn't eat yesterday either. If you don't eat you'll lose your strength," came her mother's voice from next to him.

Sadako seemed to think a minute before she said, "I'd like some *ochazuke*."

At some point Masahiro and Mitsue had slipped into the room. Mitsue, now in third grade, had ridden here on the back of Mr. Nomura's bicycle. Mr. Nomura stood guard over his student near the door, even as her life faded before his eyes.

"Masahiro," said Shigeo, "go to the shop out front and buy some rice and pickles."

At his father's words, Masahiro nodded silently and leapt out of the room. Passing him at the door, a few relatives who lived in the city rushed in saying, "Sada-chan . . ." They immediately sensed the atmosphere and fell silent.

A moment later, Masahiro was back with the bowl of hot rice and tea. Her father raised a spoonful of it to her lips. Holding a bite in her mouth, she moved her jaws slowly. "It's good," she murmured.

Then she sighed deeply. The strength left her eyelids and her open mouth seemed to move slightly.

In her fading consciousness, she was listening to the clacking sound of a streetcar. Clickety-clack, clickety-clack. The echo of the heavy wheels was getting louder, filling her head. "What? I'm back in my Hatchobori house. I was never sick," she thought. "Crackle, crackle." Bluish-white flashes sent showers of sparks into the pitch darkness. She watched, spellbound, as the showers died out, one by one.

Taking her pulse, Dr. Numata ran his eyes over his watch. Then he placed her arm over her chest and stood. Silently, he bowed to the members of the Sasaki family.

On October 25, 1955, at 9:57 A.M., twelve-year-old Sadako Sasaki passed into the sleep from which there is no awakening.

Part II

6

Those Left Behind

I

The Unity Club members who went to Noboricho Junior High School heard about the death of Sadako Sasaki around lunch time. Fumiko Yamamoto later wrote this account of what happened:

> I was playing after lunch when Haraguchi-san, who had been in sixth grade with us, came up and said, "Yamamoto-san, I heard Sasaki-san died this morning."
> "She really died?" I hoped it was a lie.
> "She really died."
> After school that day, everyone in the club got together and hurried to Sasaki-san's home. There we were told that Sasaki-san's remains were at a temple so we headed over there.

This account captures the amazement of the Bamboos well. For friends who had visited Sadako only rarely after the summer holiday, the news must have been a terrible shock.

After an autopsy at the ABCC, Sadako's remains were moved to a temple called Shinkoji in Sorazaya-cho (now Tokaichi-machi), across the river from the Sasaki home in Motomachi. The autopsy showed that Sadako's body had been completely infiltrated by leukemia. Her thyroid (a gland in the lower front part of her throat) also turned out to be cancerous. Only rarely, and then usually among the elderly, is any other cancer found along with leukemia. The ABCC had no record of any other case involving a child.

It was after Sadako's case was reported that a connection between thyroid cancer and A-bomb exposure came to light. A survey conducted by the ABCC from 1958 to 1959 found twelve cases of thyroid cancer in Hiroshima. Ten of those were A-bomb survivors and eight had been within two kilometers of the hypo-center.

But Sadako's body was now released from its long struggle against disease. It lay in a coffin of plain wood; the face under the beautifully applied makeup seemed to smile gently.

One after another the Bamboos arrived at Shinkoji Temple. Not just those who went to Noboricho Junior High, but those who went to private schools—Yoshie Kato, Kazuko Hikiji, Hiroko Nejime, and others—also rushed to the temple as soon as they could.

Mr. Nomura's face was dark with sorrow as he entered the main hall of the temple and bowed deeply to Sadako's parents. "Have they finished the autopsy?" he asked.

"Yes, they have," said Sadako's father. "Please have a look at her. That lovely makeup makes her look like a Buddha." Mr. Sasaki led the teacher to the coffin, which lay in front of an altar.

Mr. Nomura's heart flooded with grief. Here was Sadako. She had been eating *ochazuke* just this morning. Now her eyes were serenely closed, and her face bore no trace of pain or suffering.

"Sasaki . . ." He called her name in spite of himself. He had been so close to his first class in Hiroshima. It was hard to bear the thought of even one of those students dying.

He heard sobbing behind him. He turned and saw Tomiko Yokota, Kikue Itadani, Atsuko Nomura, their eyes red from crying. And not just the girls—Shinji Miyasako, Kimiya Haguma, Hiromi Sorada and several other boys were stifling the sounds of their sobs.

"*Sensei!*" cried Fumio Kumagai angrily. "Why did Sasaki-san have to die? She didn't do anything wrong!"

"That's right," added Yoshihiro Ooka, his voice trembling. "Why her?"

The children were angry from the very core of their being. Why did Sadako have to die? What was her sin? Had she killed an American soldier? Had she even thrown a rock at an American? Had Sadako ever done the slightest thing to aid the war effort? Her death was an infuriating injustice.

Mr. Nomura lay his hands on Fumio's and Yoshihiro's shoulders, nodding to show he knew how they felt. It was all he could do.

"*Sensei!*" said Mr. Sasaki in a low but urgent voice. Mr. Nomura left the circle of children and went to him.

"When I was straightening up the things around her bed at the hospital I found this." Mr. Sasaki held out a piece of paper.

Mr. Nomura looked at the sheet completely filled with tiny numbers penciled in columns. "What is it?" he asked.

"It's a record of Sadako's blood tests. She was keeping it herself."

Mr. Nomura saw that the numbers were white, red, and hemoglobin cell counts recorded at regular intervals between February 21 and July 4, and he understood.

"I asked a nurse about it," Mr. Sasaki went on. "but she said they don't tell patients their blood cell counts, and they never said a word about leukemia or A-bomb disease to her."

"So . . ."

"I think Sadako knew what she had. She was always going down to the nurse's station to visit, so she must have been sneaking looks at her chart. For her own record."

"Is that right! So young to be paying that kind of attention to her health."

"That reminds me," Mrs. Sasaki murmured. "Sometime last summer Sadako told me she had heard that if your white blood cell count goes over 100,000, you die. She kept this record until July 4. Maybe she was watching to see if her white blood cells would go over 100,000." Sadako's mother hid her face and began to weep.

The teacher looked back at the coffin, thinking about the fierce struggle with the fear of death that had been waged in that small body. "Sadako-san was quite a girl. Quite a girl." The words seemed wrung from him.

Night had fallen before they knew it. Stars twinkled all over the sky, but none of the children made a move to leave. They stayed for the *tsuya:* when someone dies in Japan, their closest friends and relatives spend the night in a vigil around the deathbed, sharing memories to comfort the departed soul. The children were determined to linger by Sadako's side as long as they could. They never ran out of things to talk about. Every memory of elementary school had now become a memory of Sadako. They covered the picnic at Chichiyasu Ranch, the school trip, the summer training camp at Fukuoji Temple in Kabe, and the field day relay.

Now and then one of them sat in front of the coffin to light a new stick of incense. Several times Kimiya Haguma knelt near the coffin, with his palms together to pray. The body lying there seemed to glow in the light of the candle. "That's a corpse," came to Kimiya's mind, but the thought neither frightened nor repelled him.

Kimiya's house in Teppocho was next door to the former

Sasaki home, but . . . He stared at her face. He had never seen her so beautiful. He wished he had gone to see her more than once at the hospital—not that regret could help anything now.

"Hey, Haguma Onii-chan!" At the sudden sound of a childish voice, Kimiya turned around to see Sadako's younger brother Eiji standing there. The little boy looked happy to have found a familiar face in the group, and stuck his fingers in his mouth to make Kimiya laugh. He had not yet grasped the meaning of his sister's death.

"Ei-chan, you've gotten big, haven't you?" Kimiya said, patting the head of the little boy. He had not seen him since the family moved to Motomachi in May.

"Why's Sada-chan sleeping? So many friends are here to play with her. She should hurry and wake up."

"Yeah, she should."

Suddenly Eiji sucked his breath in and began to sob.

"Haguma-kun," said Masahiro. "Thanks for watching him. Here, Eiji, I'll give you some candy." He picked up his little brother and held him. Eiji sobbed in Masahiro's arms as if he would never stop.

Meanwhile, the Unity Club members were saying they would get together as often as they could on the monthly anniversary of Sadako's death. "I think the best thing we could do is visit her grave," said Toshio Yasui with authority.

"Where will Sadako's grave be?" Yoshiko Hattori asked Mr. Nomura.

"Since the Sasakis' hometown is Miyoshi, their family grave is probably there too."

Naohiko Jigo folded his arms. "Miyoshi?" he said. "That's a little far. What if we put our money together to make a grave for her ashes in Hiroshima too?" "That's a good idea," someone else said, and added, "And since she died from the *pika*, we'll have a stone shaped like a mushroom cloud."

"Don't be an idiot," said Toshio Yasui. "Do you people have any idea how much it costs to make a grave? Even renting the space costs a bundle." Toshio was full of information, as usual.

"Well," said Mr. Nomura softly, "I don't know what advice I can give you about this grave idea, not knowing the Sasaki family situation and all, but I sure think it's a good idea to get together on the monthly anniversary to comfort her soul and console her parents."

Shinji Miyasako sighed. "Yeah. We really couldn't do a thing for her, could we?"

A quiet and sorrowful funeral for Sadako Sasaki was held the following afternoon. Principal Genitsu Tanaka attended to represent Noboricho Junior High School. The principal was an enthusiastic proponent of peace education. He had been in Hiroshima on "that day" ten years ago as a rescue worker, a witness to the spectacle from hell. Even after he became principal, he told his students about the horrifying destruction whenever he got a chance.

All the children who attended the *tsuya* attended the funeral too. They said their last farewells to the girl who now lay in a coffin, surrounded by flowers. Her parents handed out the paper cranes Sadako had made as mementos to the children who came. The wings of the folded cranes rustled faintly in their hands.

II

Not everyone connected with Sadako attended her funeral. Of the sixty-one members of the Unity Club, only forty or so gathered at the temple. Few homes had telephones in those days. There was no way to contact those who lived far away and attended different schools, or those who had moved to other cities.

Ken Hosokawa learned of Sadako's death in a newspaper article on the twenty-sixth of October, the day of her funeral. The evening edition of the *Chugoku Shinbun* carried the following article:

SADAKO-SAN 14TH A-BOMB VICTIM THIS YEAR

A-bomb Disease: Stricken Last Fall

The lingering curse has claimed yet another life ten years after the bombing. This year's 14th victim was a seventh-grader taken ill last fall.

Twelve-year-old Sadako Sasaki of Noboricho Junior High School lived at 15 Teppocho in Hiroshima. On the day of the bombing, Sasaki-san was exposed at her home in Teppocho, 1.5 km. from the hypocenter, but miraculously escaped injury. . . .

(The article was wrong about both Sadako's current address and the place where she was exposed.)

Returning from school that day, Ken casually glanced at the evening paper that had just been delivered. His heart froze. According to the article, Sadako had died yesterday morning. He had had no idea she was so sick.

As a matter of fact, Ken had not visited her since the start of the second semester. "If it was gonna be like this, I should've gone to see her more often." His intense regret turned to rage. "Why didn't anyone in the club tell me she was in danger? At least they could've told me yesterday!"

"Say, why don't you go to the Sasakis to pay your respects?" his mother suggested. "If she died yesterday, the funeral was probably today."

"I'm not going," he snapped. "I don't even know where they live." He retreated to silence and shut himself up in his room. He took a card from his drawer and stared at it. It was the traditional greeting card Sadako had sent him last summer vacation. He kept that card as a treasure, and finally gave it to Sadako's mother in the fall of 1983, twenty-eight years after Sadako's death. But from the beginning, Ken avoided most of the events that had anything to do with Sadako. Later on he even kept clear of the movement to build the statue for the children of the A-bomb, even though it involved all the city schools.

Ken was not the only one who learned about Sadako's death from the newspaper. Kiyo Okura, Sadako's closest friend at the end, read and reread the article at the relative's home where she was recuperating. Once Kiyo left the hospital, she had never even visited Sadako once, after all those promises. Why had she not gone? Kiyo was not sure, but she knew the hospital repelled her, with its memories of despair and frustration. Now that Sadako had died, remorse was a painful thorn in her heart.

"Her funeral must be today. If I take a bus to her home right now, I might be able to say goodbye. I don't know exactly where her house is, but they say the barbershop is on the Motomachi bus line. I ought to be able to find it if I look. But . . . what's the use of rushing over there now? It's too late. Sada-chan died yesterday and I didn't keep my promise." Fifteen-year-old Kiyo did not succeed in getting herself to go.

It was not until a year had passed, on the eve of Hiroshima's A-bomb Memorial Day, that Kiyo went to pay her respects to Sadako and saw for the first time Sadako's death name, given to her by a priest, inscribed on the wooden mortuary tablet.

Another person who read the article carefully was a young man who lived in a small shack near the A-bomb Dome. Ichiro Kawamoto was short and thin and had conspicuously large ears. He had just gotten home after a day's work for the city in a relief program for the unemployed. He had been hauling rope baskets filled with dirt for road construction since morning, but the grueling day would not keep him from the important task that awaited him that evening. After work, he had to prepare for a small gathering to be held at the East Rimpokan Hall in Onaga-cho. He saw a connection between the newspaper article now before him and the meeting. He cut out the article carefully and placed it in the rucksack he always carried. He could see the A-bomb Dome from his window. The autumn sun falling low in the west was just beginning to dye the Dome's crumbling walls a deep orange.

The Sasakis' phone rang right after they returned from the funeral. Fujiko answered it and Ichiro Kawamoto introduced himself. He told her he had learned about Sadako's death in the evening paper and continued, "As a matter of fact, we're holding a memorial service tonight at the East Rimpokan Hall in Onaga for the first anniversary of the death of another girl who died of A-bomb disease, just like Sadako-san. I was wondering if you and your family would have time to come. Some other parents who have lost their children to A-bomb disease will be there too."

Fujiko could not respond. Her mind was filled with grief over the death of her own child. There was no room in her heart at this point for empathy with someone else's loss. It was only an hour after Sadako's funeral.

"Shigeo, what should I do?" Fujiko asked.

"Onaga's a little far, isn't it?" her husband replied, thinking. "But it does seem like a meaningful coincidence for Sadako's funeral to fall on the first anniversary of that other girl's death. If you're not too tired, why don't you show up for them, just for a few minutes? We'll clean up here ourselves."

At just after eight that evening, Sadako's picture in hand, Mrs. Sasaki arrived at the East Rimpokan Hall in eastern Hiroshima. There were already about seventy adults and children there. A short, young man in work clothes introduced himself.

"I'm Ichiro Kawamoto," he said. "I'm so sorry about Sadako-san. Please come this way."

He led Fujiko to the front of the room where there stood a picture of a girl who looked to be in about the fourth grade. The picture was surrounded by offerings of flowers.

The young man's voice rose in pitch as he addressed the gathering. "Let me introduce the mother of Sadako-san, Mrs. Sasaki. I was telling you about her earlier. She's kind enough to join us even on this day, right after her own daughter's funeral." People bowed silently in response to his words. One of the women approached.

"I'm the mother of Yoshie Iwamoto. I heard about your daughter. Such a terrible sorrow, isn't it? My daughter died on October twenty-third, just a year ago. She was nine."

Fujiko looked at the photo in the front of the room. It was the face of a young, sweet, innocent girl.

"Mrs. Sasaki," Kawamoto said quietly. "Let me put Sadako-san's photo by Yoshie-chan's, if you brought it."

Fujiko opened the little bundle of things she had with her, took out Sadako's picture, and handed it to him. He gazed at it for a moment, then put it next to the other photo on the altar. Faint sighs rose from around the room.

"Well then, let us continue the service."

Seated next to Mrs. Iwamoto, Fujiko looked around the room anew. The fifty-odd children must have been friends of Yoshie Iwamoto; the adults were probably their parents. Among all the unfamiliar faces Fujiko saw one she recognized. That big, suntanned man with the stern-looking face was definitely Kiyoshi Kikkawa, who ran a souvenir shop near the A-bomb Dome. He was nicknamed "A-bomb One" because of his terrible burn scars and because he would show the keloids on his back to tourists who asked to see them. Fujiko thought it strange that he was there.

After Mrs. Iwamoto shared memories of the daughter who had died a year ago, Fujiko talked about Sadako. Never one to whom words came easily, she paused frequently. Before long, tears were welling in her eyes, and she finally threw herself down, crying. From around the room came stifled sobs of sympathy.

A middle-aged man on her right who gave his name as Mr. Fujii spoke to her quietly. "Mrs. Sasaki, we know very well how you feel. Children are innocent, and innocent children are dying, even now, after ten years. A boy from the Hiroshima Gakuen orphanage just died too. In fact, we were just talking with children from Yaga Elementary School about building a monument for all the children who've died of A-bomb disease."

"When you say 'monument,' " said Fujiko, "you mean something like the ones in Peace Park, don't you?"

"Yes. I don't know if we could build such a great one as those, but just tonight we decided on a formal appeal to the Yaga school and its PTA."

"Is that so? That reminds me of a similar conversation the children in Sadako's class had last night."

"Really?"

"Yes. I didn't hear the details, but they were talking about wanting to build a grave shaped like a mushroom cloud."

"The shape of a mushroom cloud," the man said, thoughtfully. "Maybe we should talk to Sadako-san's friends. What do you say, Kawamoto-kun?"

"That might be a good idea. Sadako-san was a student at Noboricho Junior High, wasn't she?"

"Yes, she was enrolled there, but the teacher who meant the most to her was Mr. Nomura, her sixth-grade teacher at Noboricho Elementary."

Kawamoto nodded repeatedly as he listened. "I see. I'll go meet him before long." The meeting broke up a short while later and Fujiko was getting ready to leave. Kawamoto called out to her. "Mrs. Sasaki, you live in Motomachi, don't you? We live near there. We'd like to see you home."

Mr. Kikkawa stood behind young Kawamoto, looking large and awkward.

"This is Mr. Kikkawa."

The owner of the souvenir shop greeted her gruffly. "Pleased to meet you."

"Pleased to meet you too. My family runs a barbershop in Motomachi. I know your face very well."

"I'm sure you do. I'm always showing up in the newspaper as 'A-bomb One,' or 'The man who sells the *pika.*' "

"Do you know Mrs. Iwamoto?"

"Well, not really. I'm an organizer of the A-bomb Victims Association, along with Kawamoto-kun."

"The A-bomb Victims Association?"

"Yes. It used to be called the A-bomb Victims Rehabilitation Society. It's for people who were in the *pika* to get together and talk about their problems. People who went through the *pika* have been having such a hard time ever since, but they haven't had anyone to talk to. . . ."

Fujiko listened in silence to the man's halting speech.

" . . . because only another survivor can understand what we're going through."

Fujiko nodded emphatically.

"The thing is," Kawamoto interjected excitedly. "It'll all end if the A-bomb survivors don't talk. No one'll know what happened if those of us who lived through it keep our mouths shut. We have to tell the children especially, make them understand the horror of an A-bomb holocaust. That's what I think."

There was something comic about this exchange between the burly Mr. Kikkawa and the slight Ichiro Kawamoto. Fujiko was glad she had attended the gathering. The grief of losing her own child would never disappear, but at least there were many others who shared her sorrow and suffering. If only mutual compassion could help transform pain and sadness into something different. A tiny seed of courage sprouted in her mind.

III

Ichiro Kawamoto was born in 1929 in Peru, South America, where his parents had immigrated. When he was two years old, his father fell ill and died, and his mother brought him back to Japan.

On "that day" Kawamoto was working at the thermal power plant in Saka-cho, Aki County, a suburb of Hiroshima. Even five kilometers away from the hypocenter the blast was strong enough to knock the young man to the ground.

Some hours later Kawamoto entered the city as a member of a rescue team organized at the plant. He saw heaps of burnt bodies scattered throughout the scorched city. In the days that followed he saw scene after scene he would never forget.

Then, on August 10 an incident changed the course of this sixteen-year-old's life. Four days after the bombing, exhausted by daily rescue work, Kawamoto and the rest of the team decided to get on the truck and go back to Saka-cho earlier than usual. As the truck passed a pile of bodies waiting to be cremated, Kawamoto met the eyes of a face in the pile. So burnt that even the outline of his or her features was unclear, and sandwiched among bodies that were piled like logs, the person was nevertheless clearly alive and looking at Kawamoto. The only unblackened parts of the face were the white eyes slowly following the moving truck.

"Hey, that one's still alive!"

The soldiers cremating the bodies on the street did not seem to understand the young man yelling from the truck. Kawamoto then shouted to the driver. "Please stop! Someone's about to be burned alive! Cremated alive!"

But the truck just drove faster. None of the other men on the truck paid any attention to his cries or backed up his request to the driver.

That night at their lodgings, Kawamoto attacked his fellow workers with questions.

"Why didn't you help me stop the truck?"

"Look, we're all completely beat," they answered, looking tired and gloomy. "Please, just let it go. Even if that person was alive, he or she would have died soon anyway. We couldn't have done a thing."

But sixteen-year-old Ichiro Kawamoto could not ease his torment with that thought.

"That person was still alive. Man or woman, I don't know, but that black, charred person was about to be burned alive with the other bodies. And I couldn't stop it."

This wound in his heart has remained raw ever since, bleeding from time to time.

A week later, his own body was attacked by acute radiation poisoning. He was ravaged by fever, vomiting, diarrhea, and bleeding from the gums. In the bath, his hair fell out and lay on the water like seaweed. He thought God was angry at him and that he would have to die suffering hellish pain, just like the one he could not save. Many times he decided to commit suicide, but he never actually tried. He now believes he lacked the courage to die.

He eventually recovered from the radiation sickness, but no amount of time would heal the wound in his heart. Over fifty years old now, Mr. Kawamoto still cannot eat fish served whole without the head and internal organs removed. His body revolts at the reminder of another smell that never leaves his nostrils for long—the stench of cremating bodies.

In addition, he never applied for the "A-bomb Survivor's Health Book." To possess the health book is to be labeled a "*hibakusha*" an A-bomb survivor, with disturbing finality. A surprising number of survivors shrink from the health book for that very reason.

The month following the bombing set the course and meaning of Ichiro Kawamoto's life. While trembling with fear for his own health, he dedicated himself completely to helping survivors. Ever since, with no ulterior motive, he has helped survivors in simple, practical ways. He has picked up medicine from doctors for those who find it hard to get around. He has spent all night massaging the body of a survivor in pain. He has been a constant companion to elderly, isolated survivors. And all this before "volunteering" became a well-known concept. Totally without support, alone in a small corner of the confused, postwar Japanese society, he has spent most of his waking hours helping survivors in one way or another.

He quit his job at the power plant in Sakacho and became a day laborer in order to get control of his free time. During that period Kawamoto always had several survivors depending on him for survival, and it was for their sakes that he lived in the small shack near the A-bomb Dome, depending on each day's day corps wages for that day's food. With what free time he had, he helped them in any way he could. The truth is, the rescue effort he began on August 6, 1945, has never ended.

In 1955 his heart was blazing with another new idea: a statue for the children of the A-bomb, to memorialize young lives still being claimed by the A-bombing—built not by adults but by children themselves.

In no time the twenty-six-year-old Kawamoto was seized body and soul by this plan. He had always loved children and often participated in local YMCA visits to orphanages and homes for single mothers and children. Now, two images had fused in Kawamoto's mind: one was the statue discussed at the gathering for the first anniversary of the death of fourth-grader Yoshie Iwamoto; the other was a grave shaped like a mushroom cloud, as suggested by Sadako's classmates. The statue was not an impossible dream if the children of Yoshie's Yaga Elementary, Sadako's Noboricho Junior High, and Noboricho Elementary would cooperate on the project.

For better or worse, Kawamoto always carried out any idea he thought of right away. The day after he met Sadako's mother at the memorial gathering for Yoshie Iwamoto at the East Rimpokan Hall, he visited the office of the principal at Noboricho Junior High School.

Principal Genitsu Tanaka was quite flustered by Kawamoto's sudden appearance, and was even more surprised when he heard what the enthusiastic young man had to say.

"Sadako-san was a student here. Her death is a sorrow for the whole school. What do you say, sir? Why don't Yaga and Noboricho Elementary and your school put together a joint effort to build a monument? A statue for the children of the A-bomb."

"Hmm . . ."

Shifting his glasses slightly, Mr. Tanaka surveyed Kawamoto slowly from head to toe. Who was this young man who had introduced himself as Ichiro Kawamoto? The truth was that the words pouring feverishly from the mouth of this unimpressive-looking young stranger in the worn jacket had thrown him off balance.

Unquestionably, Mr. Tanaka had also been deeply moved by Sadako's death. Attending her funeral yesterday and seeing the girl in the coffin for the first time had been a terrible shock that would never go away. She was a student at his school, but she never once passed through the doors. For a teacher and student to first meet like that, it was cruel. Too cruel. Now, here was a suggestion for a monument for Sadako and the many other children who had died. Built, moreover, by the concentrated efforts of the children in Hiroshima. Mr. Tanaka was not in the least opposed to Mr. Kawamoto's idea, but as a principal responsible for a school, he felt it appropriate to respond evasively.

"I understand your idea very well, Mr. Kawamoto, but I can't arbitrarily commit our school to this project. I must ask the teachers for their opinions and sound out the PTA and the Board of Education on the matter."

"You're right. I hope you'll take it into consideration."

Kawamoto bobbed his head of unkempt hair.

"Well then, how can I contact you? Can I have your phone number at work?"

Kawamoto shook his head slightly. "I'm working in the day corps, so I'll just come back again, if that's all right."

Mr. Tanaka was at a loss for words. "Day corps" was a short way of referring to the city and prefectural relief programs for the unemployed. The young man before him appeared to be in his late twenties, but he had no steady job. And here he was, talking about building a monument for the children who died of the A-bomb. Even more confusing, he seemed quite sincere and without ulterior motive.

After Kawamoto left, the principal leaned against the chair and looked out the window. Students were romping in the schoolyard, carefree, laughing at one another under the autumn sun. Sadako Sasaki might have been among them. If the A-bomb had not dropped on Hiroshima ten years ago, Sadako would have been dashing about too, her braids shining in the autumn sunlight.

"A statue for the children of the A-bomb," Mr. Tanaka muttered softly.

IV

A few days after Ichiro Kawamoto visited Noboricho Junior High, the movement to build a statue for the children of the A-bomb met its first crisis. Yaga Elementary School was destroyed by fire. The students, teachers, and parents of Yaga Elementary were no longer in a position to make their plans concrete. Their most urgent task was to rebuild their school.

The fire at Yaga Elementary was a shock for Kawamoto too. The central force for creating the statue for the children of the A-bomb had been blown apart. Nothing remained but to persuade Sadako's school, Noboricho Junior High, to become the nucleus of the movement.

Around that time, Kawamoto obtained a valuable piece of information. The National Conference of Junior High School Principals would be held in Hiroshima the coming fall. The chairman of the conference would be none other than Principal Tanaka of Noboricho Junior High.

It was reported that around 2,000 junior high principals from all over Japan would participate in a three-day conference from November 10 to November 12, Thursday to Saturday. The conference was only a week away.

Kawamoto rushed to the principal's office again. "What do you say, sir?" the young man urged. "Could you make an appeal for the statue at the conference? Then we could get help from junior high school students all over Japan."

But Mr. Tanaka's answer was not what Kawamoto wanted to hear.

"Mr. Kawamoto," he said. "You make it sound simple, but do you have any concrete plans? Where will you put this monument? How big will it be? How will you raise funds? Who will be responsible?"

Kawamoto could not answer. He had no blueprint, only a strong desire to help children raise a memorial with their own hands.

"One more thing," said the principal. "And this is the most important. If children are going to build the monument, the cry has to come from them. If their desire is strong enough, we have ways to help them along. But right now, I don't hear anything from any children."

After a few moments Mr. Kawamoto stood up slowly.

"I understand. When you see a proposal, and it comes from children, you'll get behind it. Is that right?"

"I can't promise for sure, but I'll consider it."

After he left the junior high, Kawamoto headed directly for Noboricho Elementary School and Mr. Nomura. This would be his first meeting with the teacher Mrs. Sasaki had told him about. Mr. Nomura was the last hope.

"A Statue for the Children of the A-bomb?" Mr. Nomura tilted his head as he listened to Kawamoto. "If that's what you call it, the name will have two prepositions, won't it?"

"What?"

"Well, I'm a little concerned about having two prepositions— 'for' and 'of'—in the name. It seems too long. Oh well, maybe it doesn't matter."

"Whatever the name turns out to be, what do you think about the idea?" Kawamoto kept his eyes on Mr. Nomura's unguarded face.

"Personally, I think it would be a very good thing. Sadako Sasaki was my pupil. I don't want any more of my kids to go through what she went through. But I wonder what the kids themselves will say." He took out his appointment book. "November eighth will be exactly two weeks after Sadako's death. The class is going to have a memorial service at the Sasakis'. Would you like to join us?"

"November eighth? That's two days before the Principals' Conference." Kawamoto thought for a minute, then nodded deeply and said, "Okay. I'll be there."

"After all, such a huge project would be impossible unless the kids really commit themselves to it. I guess I shouldn't say this, but you're quite an odd person, aren't you?" Mr. Nomura chuckled.

Ichiro Kawamoto smiled wryly.

On the evening of November 8 children wearing school uniforms gathered in twos and threes at the Sasaki barbershop on the Motomachi bus street. They were members of the Unity Club, formerly the sixth-grade Bamboo class. While most were from Noboricho Junior High, some, like Hiroshi Ueno and Motoshi Nakahara, went to other schools.

They removed the chairs and spread straw mats around on the shop's dirt floor. Then they recited the Buddhist lotus sutra in front of Sadako's picture. They had learned this sutra camping at Fukuoji Temple in Kabe during the summer of sixth grade. Sadako had been at the camp too.

When they finished the recitation, each child offered incense, and Mr. Nomura stood up.

"It's been fourteen days since Sasaki-san died. We want to share our memories of her tonight. But first, Mr. Ichiro Kawamoto here is going to show us some pictures taken at the World Conference against A- and H-bombs held in Hiroshima this last summer."

The rather small young man who had been briskly setting up for the meeting stood and turned on a slide projector. Although the children knew that such a conference had been held in Hiroshima, most of them were indifferent and found the slides boring. Kawamoto explained the slides one by one as if he were telling a story to small children. The children were more curious to know why this strange young man was here at a meeting of the Unity Club.

After the slides, the light was turned back on and it was time to talk about Sadako.

Shigeo Sasaki spoke first. "You may know that our business hasn't been doing too well. We had to sell our shop in Hatchobori and move to this shabby place. It seemed to me that Sadako's condition worsened along with our finances. I regret so much that she passed away before we could do everything we could as parents. I just hope all of you will grow up safe and sound."

The Unity Club members ached. They had done nothing for Sadako. They had formed groups to visit her before graduation, but look how that determination had faded into thin air. They had not even known how sick she was at the end. That fact pushed heaviest against their hearts.

"You know, we really didn't do anything for Sasaki-san," one boy whispered.

"Speaking of that," Mr. Nomura glanced at the young man. "Mr. Kawamoto, who showed us these slides, has something to say to you. He helps with the Youth Department at the YMCA, so some of you may already know him."

Ichiro Kawamoto gazed around at the children. His eyes seemed tired.

"As Mr. Nomura said, I came here to consult with you. This is my idea. . . ."

Kawamoto seemed comfortable talking to children and adopted a familiar tone. He gave them the background of the idea and proposed that they build a memorial for all the children who had died because of the A-bomb.

"Have you heard of the book called the *Children of the A-bomb*? It's a collection of compositions by *hibakusha* school children, edited by a teacher named Mr. Arata Osada."

"Yeah, I know." Voices piped up here and there. "I've seen the film."

"That was an important book, but now we're thinking how good it would be if we could all build a statue for the children of the A-bomb, to console the spirits of friends like Sadako-san who died because of the A-bomb. It would be meaningless if the monument were built by grown-ups, so I'm wondering if it's possible for you children to build it. That's why I came to talk to you."

V

A memorial for the children who died from the A-bomb. Forgetting their questions about who this young man was, the fascinated children found themselves listening attentively to his plan. In later years they sometimes wondered why they had agreed so easily to a stranger's proposal. Perhaps building a memorial sounded something like the greenhouse construction project they remembered from elementary school.

After his explanation, Kawamoto looked around at the children as if to gauge their response. The thirty-odd junior high students just looked at one another for a while.

"Okay. Let's do it." It was Nobuhiko Jigo who answered.

"You're pretty quick to jump on board," his brother Naohiko put in. "You sure we can do it?"

"Sure? How could I be sure? But we won't know if we don't try, right?"

"You may have a point there," nodded Toshio Yasui.

"But even if we all chip in, we'll hardly have anything. I bet a memorial in Peace Park'll cost more than a million yen."

"More than a million yen?" screeched Kikue Itadani.

"We can't do it by ourselves," said Fumio Kumagai slowly. "How about collecting contributions? Going around to schools in the city? And we'll go downtown like the people in those community fund drives you hear about. We'll say 'Please help us.'"

Then Mr. Kawamoto raised his hand. "Well, actually, if you really want to do it, there's a good way. Starting from the tenth of November, there'll be a conference here of junior high school principals from all over the country. You've heard about it, right? How about passing out leaflets at the conference hall? I hear two thousand teachers are coming. If you could get them to help, they could do a lot."

"Good idea," said Hiroko Nejime. "Two thousand principals means two thousand schools would get our leaflets. Passing them out at the hall would be great for the plan, and we wouldn't have to pay postage." Everyone nodded at Hiroko's supportive suggestion.

"If we're going to do it, we'd better hurry and make the leaflets. Otherwise we will miss our chance. Two thousand leaflets—that's a huge number, isn't it?"

"We can do it quick if we use the mimeograph. The main thing is, what'll we say?"

When it was actually time to get moving, there was a lot to do. The children decided they would print the leaflets at their old elementary school. Also, each child would contribute twenty yen to buy the paper.

"Okay then," said Mr. Kawamoto. "I'll talk to the principal and arrange for the leaflets to be distributed. Anyway, let's do our best and see what happens."

The children nodded enthusiastically.

"Mr. Nomura," said Mr. Sadaki softly. "I don't mean to object but somehow it makes me feel bad that they'll be going to so much trouble for our daughter."

"No, no. They want to do something. Sadako-san died and they are left behind. I think they're really anxious to throw themselves into some kind of action. And by chance, their energy is getting tied up with Mr. Kawamoto's proposal."

"But I wonder if it'll work out. I know there have already been lots of attempts to build memorials, and most of them don't seem to work out. Don't you think this is all going to put the children to a lot of trouble?"

"Well, we can't rule that out," Mr. Nomura said, and then he smiled. "But, as Jigo says, we won't know until we try."

After school on November 11, members of the Unity Club assembled at Noboricho Elementary School. Ichiro Kawamoto had obtained permission from Principal Tanaka to distribute the leaflets at the hall. The junior high school principals' conference had started the day before, and they only had Saturday—tomorrow—left.

The children put their heads together and finished writing the leaflet.

Let's Build a Statue for the Children of the A-bomb.

We wish to announce our desire to the principals gathered here from all over the country.

Sadako Sasaki-san, a close friend of ours, died on October twenty-fifth of A-bomb disease. We knew her since we were small. We studied and played together and enjoyed each other's company. An innocent child, Sadako-san suddenly fell sick in January this year and died after suffering for nine long months. We cannot help feeling sad for Sadako-san who knew the A-bomb in her heart and died. But since there is nothing we can do about it, at least we wish to console the spirits of all the children who have died in the same way by building a statue for the children of the A-bomb.

Please make our appeal to our friends at junior high schools all over the country and win their support.

We want this message to be told to junior high students by you, their principals. We came here especially to request this.

Hiroshima Municipal Noboricho Junior
High School 7th-Graders
All the classmates of the late Sadako Sasaki

When they completed printing the 2,000 leaflets in a school classroom, it was already past 8:00 P.M. The finished leaflets were not impressive. The ink of the blue letters was blurred here and there, and the composition was by no means a very good one. In the first place, not one concrete thing was said about what kind of statue they wanted to build. Also, it was not clear what they wanted from the junior high students all over the country. Were they asking for donations? For someone to volunteer to carry out such a campaign? But in a sense the pamphlet had to be vague. Sadako's friends simply wanted to build a statue. They had no concrete image of it and had not come up with a specific plan for getting it built. It was beyond them to think of organizing a fund-raising body or to imagine that junior high students who supported their idea might actually send money. In that sense, it was a very honest piece of writing.

And it was not just the children who were poorly prepared. Neither Kawamoto who proposed the plan nor Mr. Nomura who offered advice had thought that far ahead. They were still groping, wanting people at least to know that a group of children in Hiroshima wanted to build a statue for the children of the A-bomb. If other children were interested, the next step was to organize a campaign.

Another odd thing about the leaflets was that the children signed it "Noboricho Junior High School 7th-Graders," instead of "The Unity Club." Not all of Sadako's classmates now went to Noboricho Junior High; some went to private junior high schools, and in fact, some of the latter were there at Sadako's second-week memorial when the statue was first discussed. Surely it would have been more appropriate to sign the pamphlet "Unity Club," or "Former Noboricho Elementary School 6th-Grade Bamboo Class," or simply "Classmates of the late Sadako Sasaki."

No one has ever clearly explained why they used the name "Noboricho Junior High School 7th-Graders," but there are possible reasons. Using the name of a junior high school on a pamphlet intended for junior high principals would be helpful. Any responses would naturally be sent to the junior high school. Also, it was appropriate to mention the name of the school where Sadako was registered. Besides, Mr. Kawamoto and Mr. Nomura probably thought that if this movement were actually to be organized, Noboricho Junior High School, where Sadako had been registered, might become the nucleus. That would be the most desirable thing to happen. However, it can certainly be said that the whole nature of the movement to build a statue for the children of the A-bomb changed right from the beginning because of that one phrase, "Noboricho Junior High School 7th-Graders." For the record, it should be noted that there were some children, though few, who were going to schools other than Noboricho Junior High School and who gave all they had to the movement.

Eventually, the "Statue for the Children of the A-bomb" would be built by an organization called the "Hiroshima Children and Students Association for the Creation of Peace" (hereafter referred to as "Association for Peace"), composed of elementary, junior high, and senior high school students, mainly from Hiroshima City. But it was Sadako's classmates who initiated the movement when they petitioned the principals' conference. And they made that petition not as Noboricho Junior High School 7th-Graders but as the former sixth-grade Bamboo class of Noboricho Elementary School, in other words, the Unity Club.

From that point on, the whirling storm of the statue movement would mire Sadako's classmates in various emotional conflicts. The source of those conflicts lay already in the 2,000 leaflets they printed that night, which left their hands and faces smeared with blue ink. As soon as those leaflets were printed, the movement to build a statue for the children of the A-bomb left the Unity Club behind and attached itself to the Hiroshima Municipal Noboricho Junior High School 7th-Graders; but neither Mr. Kawamoto nor Mr. Nomura, nor certainly any of the children, had noticed that change.

7

Overcoming the Grief

I

Near the heart of the city, the Ota River divides. The east branch becomes the Motoyasu River and the west branch becomes the Hon. Between these branches lies a triangular section of the delta called Nakajima. During the Edo period Nakajima became quite a prosperous section of town and continued to flourish up through the prewar period when it consisted of Tenjin-machi, Zaimokucho, Motoyanagicho, and other neighborhoods.

On August 6, 1945, all of these neighborhoods vanished in an instant, leaving behind nothing but deserted rubble. Seven years later in 1952, the area was resurrected as Peace Memorial Park, bordered on the north by the T-shaped Aioi Bridge and on the south by Hundred Meter Boulevard.

The Hiroshima City Auditorium stood at the south end of the park, next to the Peace Memorial Museum. This large, iron and concrete building with its unique saddle-shaped roof was to be the site for the general sessions of the National Junior High

School Principals Conference. Although Kenzo Tange had helped plan the entire park and designed the other buildings, the city auditorium was designed by Toshio Shibata and was completed in March 1955. It comprised a hotel and large lecture hall designed to accommodate various large events held in Hiroshima.

On Saturday, November 12, 1955, the principals were about to conclude their conference with a general session at the auditorium. At a little past noon, eight junior high students appeared at the entrance carrying 2,000 leaflets. They also held in their arms pictures of children who had died of late effects of the A-bomb, including Sadako Sasaki and Yoshie Iwamoto. Mr. Kawamoto had borrowed the photographs from their families the day before and had them enlarged for today.

The entrance was on the second floor and faced west. It stood at the end of a path that wound gently upward from the south end of the building. When the eight students walked through the entrance, the teachers at the reception desk stared at them suspiciously.

Toshio Yasui took off his cap and greeted them. "Um ... we've got the leaflets. Thank you for letting us leave them with you."

"Leaflets?" asked one of the male teachers. "What leaflets?"

"What? Uh ... well, we're students from Noboricho Junior High and ... our principal told us we could pass these out here." Toshio had thought he had only to mention the leaflets and the teachers would take care of the rest, but the man continued to stare at him doubtfully. Teachers from their own school would have been easy to approach, but the two or three around the reception area were all from other schools.

"Let me have a look at those, uh, leaflets." At this invitation Naohiko Jigo, who had been waiting behind Toshio, opened up his cloth parcel and drew out a leaflet.

" 'Let's Build a Statue for the Children of the A-bomb'?" the teacher read out loud. "What's this? You want to pass out something like this to all these principals?"

"We have Principal Tanaka's permission to ask for help from the principals here from all over the country," answered Fumiko Yamamoto, glaring at the teacher. "He said he'd talk to the teachers at the reception desk for us. That's what he said."

Leaflet in hand, the man turned toward the female teacher behind him. "Do you know anything about this?"

"No."

Glancing back and forth from the leaflets to the children's faces, she shook her head.

The eight children were growing nervous. The lunch break was evidently ending. Elderly men who looked like they had just finished lunch walked past them and disappeared through an inner door. The afternoon session would start soon. A middle-aged man who had been chatting in a corner walked toward them. The reception teacher asked him, "Mr. Nakamura, did you get any message from Principal Tanaka of Noboricho? Some students from Noboricho are here saying they want to pass out these leaflets."

The middle-aged man turned around slowly, looking at each one of the children. "Now that you mention it, Mr. Tanaka did say something about some students who might push their way into this meeting with leaflets. He asked us to help them out. So you're the ones he was talking about, huh? You want to build an A-bomb memorial, right?"

Finally, a teacher who knew what they were talking about! The children sighed with relief. "Yes, and we'd like these passed out to all the principals."

The man glanced at his watch and said, "The afternoon session will be starting soon. Why don't you pass them out when it's over?"

"Which means?"

"When it's over at three, all the principals will come out. Oh, and do it out front, will you?"

It was not even one yet. They had more than two hours to wait.

"Now you know what to do, so wait outside, please," said the man at reception, shooing them out of the hall like chickens. "If you wait in here you'll get in the way."

"Rats!" grumbled Kiyoshi Yamamoto. "Three o'clock! Too bad we got here so early."

"Kawamoto-san made it sound like if we got here early the teacher in charge would pass them out in the meeting," said Tomiko Yokota.

"And I was nervous because I thought we'd be up on stage talking to principals from all over the country!" laughed Yoshiko Hattori.

The group walked single-file down the concrete path into the Peace Park. It was not much of a park yet, with only the museum and cenotaph breaking up the wide expanse of empty ground. Barely transplanted saplings only two or three meters tall poked up forlornly from the yellow grass.

"This is boring just sitting here," said Yoshihiro Ooka. "Let's fix the places that didn't print well."

At this suggestion, they sat down in the grass in front of the auditorium and began retracing, one by one, the places where the ink had come out too thinly on the leaflets.

"What? What happened? You haven't passed out the leaflets yet?"

Eight faces looked up to see Ichiro Kawamoto in front of them, wearing a YMCA jacket and a baseball cap.

"We have to wait until three," complained Atsuko Nomura.

"That's strange. They were supposed to be passed out for you during the lunch break."

Kawamoto looked perplexed and headed up to the entrance.

Soon he was back, grumbling, "Irresponsible. It looks like Mr. Tanaka didn't get the message across. Sorry, but wait until the meeting's over, okay?"

"It's okay. We already decided to do that," answered Naohiko sullenly.

Kawamoto joined the circle and began going over leaflets with his pencil.

"Kawamoto-san, do you have the day off today?" asked Kiyoshi.

"Not exactly. In the day corps, you can take off whenever you want. Of course, you don't get paid when you don't work."

The children, who had not known until that moment what he did for a living, stared at him with an odd feeling. Seventh-graders understood that "day corps," or "day corps programs for the unemployed," meant daily labor provided by the city and prefectural governments to people who didn't have jobs. It was mostly physical work, like road construction or weeding in parks. Since the government paid 254 yen a day, the laborers were called "Ni-ko-yons"— which means "Two-five-fours."

The children thought of the laborers in the programs as people who had lost their jobs, society's failures. How could such a young man be reduced to this? And how could someone with no steady work take such an interest in helping them? They were completely baffled.

"Oh, yeah!" said Kawamoto, as if he just thought of something. "Today I brought my camera, so I could take a picture of all of you." Lifting a camera out of his sack, he asked a passing tourist to take their picture. The group lined up, holding the pictures of Sadako and the other children. Mr. Nomura too had always whipped out his camera whenever anything special happened. Maybe this young man had the same habit. All in all, the children were feeling quite peculiar.

Finally it was three o'clock. Once again they climbed the

slope to the entrance of the auditorium. Standing on the veranda in front of the building, the eight children waited for the conference to end. Soon the double doors at the other end of the lobby swung open left and right, and the participants walked out carrying their briefcases. Principals from all over the country.

"Now, let's bow politely as we pass them out," Naohiko reminded the others.

When the first man walked past, Naohiko called out loudly, "Please take this and read it. Please!" and bowed, as if to demonstrate. The man, who was wearing a coat and shouldering a large bag, looked at Naohiko in some surprise and began reading the leaflet as he continued down the slope. The principals continued to file out, more than 2,000 of them. In the center of the stream outside the door stood the students, frantically handing out leaflets.

They had no time to study the effect the leaflets were having. At last the wave died down to a trickle, and they could look around. A gray-haired principal was gazing at the pictures of Sadako and the other victims, which the girls held in their arms. Another man wearing glasses stopped part-way down the path and stood reading the leaflet. Another turned back toward them and approached purposefully. "Were you all friends of Sadako Sasaki-san?"

"Yes," Naohiko answered nervously.

"Were you exposed to the bomb too?"

"What? Yes."

"Did all your family survive?"

"No, my older brother who was in junior high died."

The principal stared at the boy a little while. "I see. I'll definitely tell everyone about the statue for the children of the A-bomb. Keep up the good work and take care of yourself. Here, this isn't much, but . . ." The balding, slightly heavy man drew several 100-yen bills from his wallet and pressed them into

Naohiko's hand. Then, with a swing of his briefcase, he slowly set off down the slope.

When the last principal came out of the building, the children were completely out of leaflets. "Well, well, it's over," said Naohiko, swinging his arms.

"I'm starved," said Kiyoshi, grimacing under his glasses. Suddenly, they all noticed their empty stomachs. That morning at school they had waited impatiently for the last period to end so they could dash out of the building. No one had eaten lunch.

Yoshiko bent down and picked up a crumpled leaflet that had been thrown there. "I wonder . . . will they really go back and tell people about this?" Could the man who tossed it have read what was said on it?

When they rounded the curve to the south, they saw two disabled veterans standing under the Peace Memorial Museum. One played the accordion; the other held a collection box in his artificial hand and bowed to the tourists who emerged from the museum from time to time. Their white robes swayed gently in the twilight breeze as the notes to the song "Senyu," Comrades in Arms, reverberated off the museum wall.

II

The children had placed leaflets in the hands of most of the junior high principals in the country. Would they read them? Would they plead their case to the children in their schools? Would some of those students give their support to the plan?

The days following the conference were a mixture of anxiety and anticipation for the Unity Club members. They had no way of knowing that Principal Tanaka had spoken about Sadako in front of the 2,000 principals during the general session. Mr. Tanaka had not responded warmly to the idea of a statue for the children of the A-bomb; nor did he actively support the seventh-graders' passing out leaflets at the front doors. He merely mentioned to a few teachers that some students from his school might appear wanting to leaflet and asked that they be allowed to do so.

This is not to suggest that Mr. Tanaka was unconcerned about the A-bomb. As a matter of fact, whenever August 6 drew near, the principal mounted the platform and spoke to his students about the terrible suffering of that day. And at the conference, when he greeted the principals as host, he told of a student in his school, Sadako Sasaki, who had died two weeks ago. He pleaded for teachers to work to keep such a disaster from occurring again.

Although he did not mention the statue, Mr. Tanaka's impassioned account of the girl who had died of A-bomb disease struck the hearts of his listeners. Then, when they left the building, they were handed leaflets that said "Let's Build a Statue for the Children of the A-bomb." The leaflets were signed, "Noboricho Junior High 7th-Graders, All the Classmates of the Late Sadako Sasaki." Anyone reading the leaflets would assume that they were connected to Principal Tanaka's plea, and that his entire school was involved in the statue idea. The leafletting at the entrance had proven to be timely.

Actually, at the time of the principals' conference, only a few students and teachers at Noboricho knew anything about the leafletting. Two or three teachers had heard fragments of the idea from their principal or from Sadako's classmates. Yukio Matsuura was one of those few. He was an English teacher born in 1922. A soldier stationed in China at the war's end, he returned to Japan a few years later. Although he never saw the devastation of Hiroshima with his own eyes, it was impossible for him to live in this city and not be touched by the bombing. Because his lodgings were near the Sasaki home in Teppocho, he had seen Sadako around the neighborhood since she was a small girl. Her older brother Masahiro was now his student. It pained him deeply that Sadako had died before she had spent one day in junior high school.

After classes one day near the end of November, he saw one of his students, Yukiko Hiraoka, crying in the hall. "What's wrong, Hiraoka?" he asked.

Sobbing, she replied, "It's almost the first month anniversary of Sada-chan's death, and we want to have a meeting, but we can't find a place to do it." The forty members of Mr. Nomura's class who had gone on to Noboricho could not get together without borrowing a classroom.

"What? Why didn't you tell me before? Use my room." He pushed up his thick glasses and smiled at her.

This encounter led Sadako's former classmates to form a group they eventually named the "Kokeshi Club." The former Bamboos now at Noboricho Junior High began to use Mr. Matsuura's classroom, and his interest in their activities grew. This deepened his friendship with the Sasakis, who began to consult him on various matters.

It would be easy to say that Mr. Matsuura was the type who just liked to help people, but helping a group of children who were neither in his class nor in any club that he advised could not have been an easy thing. Although the term "entrance exam wars" was not in use then, teachers had their hands full coping with their fifty students, not to mention managing the extra study programs carried on by all junior high schools.

Later, after the statue movement had solidified into the official organization, the Hiroshima Children and Students Association for the Creation of Peace, Mr. Matsuura continued to look after Sadako's classmates, and even after the statue was completed, he remained a supportive friend to the Sasakis.

In a sense, Mr. Matsuura took Mr. Nomura's place in the lives of the Bamboos at Noboricho. Ironically, just as Mr. Matsuura was becoming involved, Mr. Nomura was parting company with the movement to build the statue. When Yoshihiro Ooka, Fumiko Yamamoto, and others told Mr. Nomura about their great success leafletting ("One of the principals even gave us money out of his own pocket!"), he felt a twinge of unease. How would their activities be interpreted by their teachers? The children's project was not some momentary whim, and they had no ulterior motive. He wondered if he should talk to the main teachers at the junior high to make sure they understood this. By the time the students finished their excited report on the principals' conference, he had made up his mind to do just that. After turning it over carefully in his own mind, he described the situation to an acquaintance who was a PTA officer at the junior high school, and asked for his help.

"The kids can't build a statue without some help. Will you arrange for me to meet the principal and the other PTA officers? I want to explain the background of this movement."

"That's a good idea. If everyone hears the story from you, they'll know the project isn't just some crackpot idea dreamed up by children." The friend promised to act as the go-between.

But he did not keep his promise. For some reason, he did not introduce Mr. Nomura to either Principal Tanaka or the PTA president. It is not clear whether the school refused to meet with him or whether the acquaintance decided on his own not to follow through on his agreement. In either case, from that point Mr. Nomura lost all connection with the movement. It is interesting to note, though not directly related, that Sadako's own elementary school did not appear later among the names on the list of founding schools of the Hiroshima Children and Students Association for the Creation of Peace.

From the day the leaflets were distributed, Ichiro Kawamoto too was shunted away from the mainstream of the movement. The originator of the statue idea and the mastermind behind the leafletting, Kawamoto awaited the reactions to the appeal with the same mixture of excitement and anxiety the children were feeling. If the response was favorable, good; if not, they would move on to another plan. Kawamoto naively believed he would be informed of the outcome one way or another.

In fact, he never received any formal notification. He first learned of the overwhelming response to the leafletting on Christmas Eve of that year when someone stuck a copy of the "Noboricho Junior High Newsletter" No. 31 under the door of his house near the Atomic Dome. Who had delivered it? One of Sadako's classmates?

But by the time Kawamoto learned of the response to the leaflets, the movement was already undergoing enormous changes. The message of the leaflets, scrawled clumsily by twelve- and thirteen-year-olds on rough paper, had been carried far and wide in the travelcases of the principals. Some days later they had been read aloud to assembled junior high students in freezing schoolyards up north, over speaker systems at big city schools surrounded by tall buildings, and in seaside classrooms in the south.

The principals talked to their students about the young girl who had to die when she was only twelve years old. They told of the terrible photos they had seen in the memorial museum; of the fearful atomic bomb that had annihilated tens of thousands in an instant. Though they had not experienced the atomic bomb, this generation of students and teachers knew the terror and suffering of war in their bones. They understood that a statue for the children of the A-bomb would not merely be a symbol of mourning for the dead children, but a vow to maintain peace for the future.

The naive appeal printed on rough paper was creating a powerful groundswell.

III

The list of contributors to the "Statue for the Children of the A-bomb" compiled by the Association for Peace, and the

"Noboricho Junior High School Newsletter" issued on December 24, 1955, both indicate that contributions from all over Japan started arriving at Noboricho Junior High School at the end of November, within twenty days after the principals conference:

November 30: ¥1,601, Fuse Junior High School, Ochi County, Shimane Pref.

December 7: ¥1,600, Motodate Junior High School, Senboku County, Akita Pref.

December 10: ¥2,587, Yuzawa Junior High School, Minami Uonuma County, Niigata Pref.

¥1,500, Toyokita Junior High School, Toyota County, Hiroshima Pref.

December 13: ¥1,075, Joto Junior High School, Matsuyama City, Ehime Pref.

¥2,232, Wakimachi Junior High School, Mima County, Tokushima Pref.

December 15: ¥1,812, Yamashiro Junior High School, Enuma County, Ishikawa Pref.

December 20: ¥500, Otsu Junior High School, Nagaoka County, Kochi Pref.

¥1,812, Monbetsu Junior High School, Saru County, Hokkaido

December 27: ¥1,500, Toyokita Junior High Okusa Branch, Toyota County, Hiroshima Pref.

December 30: ¥ unknown, Shin Totsukawa Junior High School, Kabato County, Hokkaido.

The list shows that the first response came not from big city schools but from small schools in the country. Maybe it took longer for the large student bodies in city schools to respond to fundraising efforts, while small country schools could raise the money quickly.

The school that led the way was Fuse Junior High nestled among the Chugoku mountains of Shimane Prefecture. Very few of those students had experienced any bombing at all, and it is interesting that the first students to respond to the call of the statue movement had grown up knowing the least about war.

These schools sent significant sums of money. At that time a monthly magazine cost 100 yen. A city streetcar was 13 yen for an adult, and an average family's monthly income was barely 30,000 yen. The writer, a seventh-grader at the same time as Sadako's friends, was getting 300 yen a month for allowance. By the end of December over 14,000 yen had been received at Noboricho Junior High, the equivalent of ten times that amount today.

Along with the donations came warm messages for the statue movement. Principal Takeo Haniu of Nishi Ashibetsu Junior High School in Ashibetsu City in Hokkaido was an outstanding supporter. He promoted the movement in an article entitled "Foundation for World Peace—The Movement to Build a Statue for the Children of the A-bomb." This article was published not only in his own school newsletter but in the *Hokkaido Shinbun* as well on January 17, 1956. He continued his steadfast support until the statue was completed.

As reverberations of support for the project bounced back one after another from every corner of Japan, no one was more surprised than the Noboricho Junior High community itself. Although the idea had originated with a group of their own seventh-graders, no teacher had been involved or had even read the original leaflets. However ignorant they might be about the doings in their own backyard, they had to do something about the messages pouring in and the donations now adding up to over 10,000 yen. For the time being it was decided to entrust the money to the student council, and the responses to the messages to Sadako's former classmates.

Needless to say, the children were overjoyed watching letters from all over the country pile up in response to their call. For the most part, it was the girls in the group who penned the thank you notes, one after another. A teacher needed to supervise the running of this operation, so Yukio Matsuura became the pipeline between the school and Sadako's classmates. At the time Mr. Matsuura had no great vision of the project. He had simply offered his classroom to a group of Sadako's classmates, some of whom happened to be his students; it was this slight connection that eventually tied him to the movement.

How did the teachers of Noboricho Junior High feel about the movement? At first, very few had a clear understanding of what was taking place. They saw a group of children raising funds for some statue, not a peace movement with the potential to unite the efforts of adults and children alike. While no teacher stood in their way, neither did any take this opportunity to raise the subject of the bomb in class, or suggest starting a club for peace studies. The only legacy of the movement in the entire school was a club begun by teacher Tetsuro Tsuchiya. A letter written in *Esperanto* had arrived from an Englishwoman who happened to be aware of the movement. Mr. Tsuchiya took the letter as an opportunity to form an Esperanto club.

Although the faculty took no active interest in the movement, Principal Tanaka worked for it enthusiastically. It is no exaggeration to say that he was putting on a one-man show. The man who had only half-heartedly cooperated during the leafletting was now looking through stacks of letters containing cash contributions and was taking decisive steps.

The word "decisive" certainly characterizes Mr. Tanaka during this period. Because he died in 1966 around the age of sixty, this writer was unable to interview him and cannot attempt to describe what was in his heart. But we know enough of the situation at that time to infer the strength of his devotion to the cause and to marvel at his vigorous and swift pursuit of the goal.

As the vice president of the Japan Junior High School Principals Association, he spent more time out of town on business trips than he did in his office. This made him the perfect person to promote a national movement. The teachers at his school did not oppose his activities. Actually, conflict between principals and teachers was extremely rare in Hiroshima during this period. When Principal Tanaka described the plan to build the statue, the teachers simply agreed to go along with the idea.

Principal Tanaka's ideas about the project were expressed in an article he wrote for the December 24 issue of the "Noboricho Junior High Newsletter":

Regarding the "Statue for the Children of the A-bomb"
Principal Genitsu Tanaka

The Conference of Junior High School Principals took place on November 11 and 12 at the Hiroshima City Auditorium. . . . During my address on behalf of local principals I made an appeal for the A-bomb victims who continue to suffer today, and for Sadako Sasaki-san in particular, a seventh-grader in our school who died of A-bomb disease. I stressed how critical it is that this terrible weapon never be used again anywhere on this planet. The members of the conference were greatly moved, and afterward letters arrived from all over addressed to the student council. One letter said, "Our principal told us that the suffering from the atomic bomb continues and that our fellow students are still succumbing, one after another. Through this contribution to the memorial statue we want to express our sympathy and offer our prayers for the peaceful repose of their souls."

The money has been pouring in, already totaling over ten thousand yen. Frankly, I was not expecting such a response, and our school did not adequately discuss or prepare a system for dealing with the money. We have entrusted it to the student council for the time being. Now we must formally approach every school in the country. This is no longer a project for Noboricho Junior High alone. This movement must become a way to mourn the war victims of every elementary, junior, and senior high school in every city. We want to approach every student or children's council in every city and help them make their project work. We will carry the heartfelt wishes of the children of Hiroshima to all the student councils everywhere and use their contributions to build a "Statue for the Children of the A-bomb."

I believe that a memorial built by the children of Japan will amaze those who visit our city from all over the Earth. It will become a symbol evoking devout prayers for peace. With the deaths of those innocent boys and girls in our minds, we wish to implement this plan on a large scale, as a prayer for the repose of the souls of the junior and senior high students falling victim one after another, year after year. This is our duty, those of us who survive, and we of Noboricho Junior High will raise the first call.

This long passage has been reprinted here because it so clearly expresses Mr. Tanaka's feelings and expectations for the movement. And since the statue movement did follow the course he predicted, we must admire his vision and ability to follow through. The only troubling aspect of this article is that nowhere does it mention the seed from which the movement sprouted, the leafletting that day by the seventh-graders. It does not acknowledge the ones who had the idea to build the statue in the first place. Anyone who did not know the facts would infer that Principal Tanaka himself had first proposed the idea at the national principals conference or that his speech had so moved the principals that they had generated the idea themselves. Since Mr. Tanaka had spoken to Ichiro Kawamoto previously and had known of the movement since its inception, these omissions are disturbing. It is unfortunate that we cannot ask Mr. Tanaka to clear up these questions.

It must be noted that this article was part of a special issue of the "Noboricho Junior High Newsletter" published on December 24, 1955, entitled "Let's Not Repeat the Tragedy—Our Prayers for a Statue for the Children of the A-bomb." Other articles in that issue told the story of the leafletting and reported that the student council had united solidly behind the movement.

At any rate, it can be said that the answer to the appeal that Sadako's classmates printed late into the night while they slurped noodles for supper came in this issue of the newsletter. Exactly two months after her death, just into winter break on December 25, the Unity Club gathered at the Sasaki home to exult in their unexpected success.

8

A Cry for Peace

I

Nineteen hundred and fifty-six was a year of change for Japan. In accordance with the U.S.-Japan Nuclear Agreement signed in November 1955, a nuclear power research institute was opened in Tokaimura, Ibaraki Prefecture in April—the first step toward the age of nuclear power. The worldwide economic upswing supported the Jimmu Boom in Japan, bringing televisions, refrigerators, and washing machines into average homes. Japan made great progress in foreign relations by restoring diplomatic relations with the Soviet Union and entering the United Nations.

The first Japanese observation team set off for Antarctica. The Japanese wrestling, gymnastic, and swimming teams performed outstandingly in the Melbourne Summer Olympics. Japan's Igaya won a silver medal in the Cortina Winter Olympics. Amid the bright events appearing one after the other in the news, an "Economic White Paper" in July declared that the postwar period was over.

Ten years after the end of the war, society was definitely in transition, as was symbolized by the youths drunk on sex and violence in Shintaro Ishihara's *Taiyo no Kisetsu* (Season of the Sun). An American movie called *The Blackboard Jungle* was released around this time. Youth unrest was not a passing phase; it pointed to a core of sickness rooted in civilization itself.

The sickness was not confined to capitalistic societies. Government upheavals in Poland and Hungary in October were followed by Soviet interventions, revealing plainly a number of contradictions within the socialist system of government.

In Hiroshima too, 1956 was a year to remember. The formation of the Japan Confederation of A- and H-bomb Sufferers Organizations (JCSO) on August 10 united the formerly separate survivor populations of Hiroshima and Nagasaki in the effort to seek aid and compensation from the national government. On September 11, the dreams of many people were realized when the Hiroshima Atomic Bomb Hospital opened its doors, adjoining the Red Cross Hospital. Since that day it has specialized in caring for those suffering late effects of the bombing.

For the "Statue for the Children of the A-bomb" movement as well, 1956 was certainly a pivotal year. The first meeting of the "Statue for the Children of the A-bomb" Preparation Committee was held on January 18 at Noboricho Junior High School and was attended by around one hundred elementary, junior high, and senior high school students from city schools. On the twenty-eighth of the month, the committee chose a name for the group, outlined its activities, and elected officers. They called the official organization responsible for building the statue the Hiroshima Children and Students Association for the Creation of Peace (Association for Peace).

The group's statement of intent, quoted from Kiyoshi Toyota's book *Habatake Senbazuru* (Fly, Thousand Cranes), and its by-laws follow:

Statement of Intent

We mourn for the souls of the children and students who were sacrificed to the war, and we wish to comfort our friends who suffered by erecting a "Statue for the Children of the A-bomb." We pledge to work toward a peaceful world that will never again wage war.

Bylaws

I. General Provisions

1. Goals and Undertakings—This organization will be composed of children and students of public and private elementary, junior high, and senior high schools of Hiroshima. With the goal of uniting our efforts to make a peaceful, livable world, we undertake the following:

a. To build the "Statue for the Children of the A-bomb."

b. To conduct workshops, discussions, and lectures to promote peace.

c. To educate people about peace through publications, surveys, and correspondence.

d. Other necessary matters.

2. Funding—These activities will be financed through outside donations and our own contributions.

3. Office—This organization will maintain an office at the Hiroshima Children's Culture Center, located at 1 Motomachi.

II. Officers

4. Types of positions and number of people in each position:

Chairman—1

Vice-chairman—2

Standing committee members—19 (representing 19 schools)

Supervisors—10

According to Kiyoshi Toyota's book, there were four advisers in addition to the positions listed in the bylaws. They were:

Hiroshima City Board of Education Section Chief of General Affairs, Morioka

Chairman of the Association of Hiroshima Elementary School Principals, Minoru Tanaka

Chairman of the Association of Hiroshima Junior High School Principals, Genitsu Tanaka

Chairman of the Association of Hiroshima Senior High School Principals, Sadao Masatsuki

The chairman of the organization itself was Motomachi High School eleventh-grader Masashi Nakamura, and the standing committee members were to be the student council heads of the nineteen participating schools. The schools that participated were:

Elementary—Niho, Minami, Honkawa, Hakushima, Funairi, Tenma, Kanzaki

Junior High—Kannon, Kokutaiji, Sanyo, Shinonome Branch (attached to Hiroshima University), Otemachi, Noboricho

Senior High—Motomachi, Yasuda, Shudo, Sotoku, Music, Koryo

There were no flaws in either the statement of intent or the bylaws. Because it is unlikely that students at that time possessed such planning ability, one senses Mr. Tanaka's efforts behind the scenes. It must have been the principal's drive, or more accurately his political skill, that guided the group to such a high level of organization within less than two months after the money began to come in.

The small number of schools, however, is puzzling. At that time public schools alone numbered forty elementary, fourteen junior high, and nine senior high schools. When private schools were added, the total number of schools in the city must have been over eighty. We can assume that each of those schools must have been approached while the organization was taking shape; only nineteen responded to the invitation. Still, the number of participating schools doubled as time went on. If the preparation committee had taken more time, Sadako's old school Noboricho Elementary (which joined the following year) and Yoshie Iwamoto's Yaga Elementary might have been among the original group.

The framework of the organization to build the statue was now completely spelled out. The movement that had begun with the sixth-grade Bamboo class was spreading to elementary, junior, and senior high schools all over the city.

Before the Association for Peace was formed, Noboricho Junior High School picked its own Japanese language teacher Kiyoshi Toyota to be its adviser. Thirty-four-year-old Mr. Toyota, born in 1921, was an experienced teacher. A newcomer to Noboricho since his transfer in October the year before, he suddenly found himself with a national movement on his hands.

Mr. Toyota had written about the atomic bombing in literary pieces for years. Through his role as editor of *Kagen*, a magazine for *tanka* (short poems) enthusiasts, he continues even today to speak out against the bombing. He must have responded warmly and enthusiastically to the idea of the "Statue for the Children of the A-bomb." He was to walk in step with the Association for Peace for the next three years.

When the drive to raise money from elementary, junior high, and senior high schools within the city ended on March 25, their coffers contained 274,345 yen. It was time to send a prospectus of the movement to schools throughout the country. The prospectus (again taken from Mr. Toyota's *Habatake Senbazuru*) is

Toward a "Statue for the Children of the A-bomb"

> After months of suffering, Sadako-san left this world. Yoshito-kun fell sick with A-bomb disease in the fourth grade and also died.
>
> Sadako-san was only two when she experienced the A-bomb. Her mother carried her on her back in a desperate flight to Kusunoki-cho, and they fortunately escaped death. But then last year at this time a symptom of A-bomb disease appeared, and she went to a doctor.

They gave her sickness the difficult name of subacute lymph gland leukemia [*sic*]. She struggled against that disease until breath failed her nine months later.

When we, her friends, visited her at the Red Cross Hospital, she lay in bed folding paper cranes out of medicine wrappers. We asked her, "What are you going to do with all those cranes you're making?" She answered reproachfully, "What do you think, I'm gonna hurry and get well." We can still see her face in that moment. Athletic Sadako-san must have wanted to get well fast and start winning races again. With everyone helping her she managed to make more than 1,000 cranes. After she died we each received a crane as a remembrance of her. Then we made them an offering by placing them around her face and chest as she lay in the coffin. Then we said "goodbye."

Yoshito-kun's condition worsened after Christmas. In the end he just lay in his bed, nodding whenever anyone asked him a question. He died on January 24. He missed being in the A-bomb film he was looking forward to.

This is a letter Sadako-san wrote while she was in the hospital:

"The blood transfusions I get through my arm are painful. The doctor said that sick people need to feel a little pain to get better. I don't care about pain, I just want to get well so I can go see you during spring break."

When someone read this aloud during our homeroom period at Noboricho, Yamaguchi-san said, "Listen, let's build a statue for the children of the A-bomb."

Yokichi-kun pointed out, "But that'll take a lot of money," and we were all stumped.

Then Yamaguchi-san said, "We'll economize and save it up," and we all agreed.

That idea came all the way down to January 28, 1956, when representatives of all the elementary, junior, and senior high students in the city gathered and resolved to erect a statue.

When the bomb dropped we were all still small. We hardly remember anything about it. But many of our older brothers and sisters were helping demolish buildings or working in factories in the city; they were among the 240,000 who perished in the bombing. They can never again know the pleasure of schoolwork, or enjoy a Carp game.

Our friend Koji-kun's mother still weeps as she tailors clothing.

Early this February, the city's Council for Countermeasures against Atomic-bomb Diseases announced that there are still 9,700 A-bomb survivors among us, which is somehow frightening. Even now adults in Hiroshima are coming down with A-bomb diseases and dying, one after another. And children like Sadako-san and Yoshito-kun who survived the bomb without a scratch and went to school right along with everyone else are closing their lives after all this time. Is it all right for things like this to happen?

We in Hiroshima were not the only ones wounded by the war. Children and students all over the country were sacrificed in one way or another—many are still in pitiful situations. Our 10,000 older brothers and sisters who perished in the A-bomb didn't want to die. How horribly they must have suffered! Even now, sometimes at night you can almost hear them crying under the bridges.

Sadako-san is dead, but she still doesn't have a Buddhist altar. Her family lives in a cold, drafty, little shack.

Friends of the country! We want to honor through our own effort the spirits of these many children, some of whom were our friends. We are saving our allowances to build a "Statue for the Children of the A-bomb." Urging each other on, we devote ourselves every day to building a financial base for this project. However, we know it will take a lot of money to build a statue that is significant and meaningful. This is our great problem. Will you encourage us, even help us? We ask you from the bottom of our hearts.

> March 1, 1956
> Hiroshima Children and
>   Students Association for the
>   Creation of Peace
> Masashi Nakamura, Chairman
> (Senior at Motomachi High School)

II

In January 1956, television test broadcasting began in Hiroshima. Television broadcasting had been carried on in Japan since 1953, so local people had already seen television sets displayed in front of electric goods stores. Now for the first time they saw the pictures moving on the TV screen.

At twilight large crowds often gathered around television sets placed on main streets and the open area in front of train stations. The start of the tests coincided with the New Year's *Sumo* Tournament, so people gazed at the grappling in the ring that they had only glimpsed on movie newsreels before. They lingered by the sets, even forgetting to go home.

Later, a hastily thrown up "TV Hall" in front of the station at Koi-machi in west Hiroshima began charging admission. Broadcasting did not begin until twilight, but eager viewers entered the "hall" an hour early to stare at the test pattern and wait for the live pro-wrestling show.

When Sadako's classmates came back to school after winter break, they too must have been buzzing with television talk. Many stores in downtown Hatchobori had bought television sets to lure customers inside, so there was no need to pay money to watch.

While the Bamboos were busy chatting about television, the groundwork for the Association for Peace was being laid. But no one told them about that. No one even notified them about January 28, when student council officers of the participating schools met at Noboricho Junior High to formally open their organization. All they heard was a rumor that a citywide group to raise money for a statue was forming, and that representatives of various schools had met on the twenty-eighth to discuss it.

"Don't you think it's strange?" This was the initial reaction of Unity Club President Nobuhiko Jigo when he heard the rumor. "Weren't we the ones who came up with the idea of a statue for the A-bomb children? You'd think they might have at least told us what's going on."

"Come on, don't get so mad about it," Fumio Kumagai

soothed him. "You read the school newsletter that came out before winter break, didn't you? The student council decided to raise the money. Noboricho can't do it alone, so they're getting other schools to help them."

"Fine. Let them get other schools. All I'm saying is, I don't get why they have to sneak around behind our backs. Do you?"

"Look," chuckled Fumio. "We're not student council officers, not one of the Bamboos is. So there's nothing we can do about it."

Nobuhiko could hardly argue with that. After all, the Bamboos were only in the seventh grade, not a glorious position in the world of junior high school.

Seventh-grade bodies are only beginning to develop, and their minds are still childish in many ways. Only rarely can seventh-graders take leadership roles in school events or club activities. Ninth-graders seem about ten years older to them; ninth-graders holding positions of responsibility in the student council are great figures of authority.

"Yeah, if student council presidents are involved, it's no place for us, that's for sure." Reluctantly, Nobuhiko sheathed his sword.

Whatever the reasons, it was hard for the Bamboos to feel connected to the movement started by the association that had formed without telling them. If they had been ninth-graders and one or two of them had joined the Association for Peace, the Bamboos might have reacted more favorably and there might not have been as much emotional friction. And if the school or student council had treated Sadako's classmates as the starting point of the movement, things might have developed differently.

These things are clear in hindsight, but Principal Tanaka and the student council had their hands full with a national fundraising effort, and had no time to consider the feelings of Sadako's friends. Many groups and individuals were working toward A-bomb memorials during this period; most of them failed to raise the necessary funds.

If adult efforts were failing, could children raise enough to build a statue? Furthermore, since this fundraising targeted whole schools instead of individuals, once money had been received, it was not possible to abandon the project. Principal Tanaka could not be expected to shoulder the entire responsibility by himself.

Another viewpoint is that Sadako's classmates had distributed their leaflets without a well-considered plan. They had created a burden which Mr. Tanaka, the student council, and the Association for Peace had shouldered.

Mr. Toyota, however, said that he was concerned about Sadako's classmates from the beginning, and tried to make them feel included. Unfortunately, his efforts got lost in the process of the movement and were never communicated to the children.

Emotional friction notwithstanding, the Association for Peace moved into high gear, and the members of the Bamboo class, especially those at Noboricho, found themselves helping out.

Before the Association for Peace formed, the student council kept the donations and letters; Sadako's classmates wrote the thank you letters. They continued to do so even after the association had taken over the other tasks.

Yukio Matsuura supervised the letter writing. Mr. Matsuura also felt a little estranged from the association. He felt sorry for the seventh-graders. The ones who had originally proposed the memorial now had no voice in the matter at all. They were merely assigned to write the letters. He wanted them to have their say too.

Before winter vacation that year, he had given them an assignment. "You all know that the movement to build the Statue for the Children of the A-bomb is gathering momentum," he told them. "Money and letters are coming in from everywhere. Why don't you write down what you're feeling about all this?"

"What should we write?" asked Shuji Kurata, cocking his head suspiciously.

"Since you know more about Sadako-san than anyone, why don't you write your memories about her?" the teacher suggested. "The human memory is an unreliable thing. Today we hardly even know what happened yesterday. That's why you always see me taking notes. Now would be a good time for you to record what you remember about Sadako-san."

"I'm terrible at compositions."

"Can we write poems?"

Voices popped up from around the room.

Finally, Mr. Matsuura put his foot down. "This is your homework for winter break. Get it?"

Mr. Matsuura was an English teacher, but he also loved Japanese literature and often tried his hand at essays. When he assigned this homework in December 1955, the Association for Peace had not yet been formed, but what little he heard in teachers' meetings warned him that the association would evolve without much connection to Sadako's classmates. In spite of his persuasive efforts, few of those classmates turned in the compositions when they came back to school in January.

"They don't care how I feel," Mr. Matsuura thought. "Why should I go out of my way for them?" But he increased the pressure. Every time he ran into one of them at school, he asked, "Hey! Where's my composition?"

By the middle of January he had managed to squeeze a little pile of compositions out of them. Predictably, once they took pen in hand, memories of Sadako began to drift to the surface. The compositions may have been poorly written, but they gripped the heart. Mr. Matsuura, a romantic, was deeply moved.

The prefectural junior high speech contest was coming up at Kumano Junior High on February 4. Mr. Matsuura promptly began to urge some of Sadako's classmates to enter. "What do you think? You can use your compositions as a base and talk about Sadako-san and the statue."

The children looked at each other. "You do it, Jigo. You always talk so big. Give it a try."

Startled, Naohiko, the older of the Jigo brothers, shook his head. "Me? I can't do it. If you want a speaker, get Fumiko." He pointed at Fumiko Yamamoto.

"Oh no you don't, not me. Yasui-kun would be good though. He likes to get up in front of people and talk."

"Not me either. I can only do *rakugo*, my funny monolog. I can't talk about anything serious."

Every one of them shied away from the prospect of entering the speech contest.

Mr. Matsuura finally gave up and asked one of his own students, Noriko Mandai. Together, the children worked their compositions into a single speech for Noriko, entitled "Pledging Peace to a Star." Noriko won top marks in voice volume, attitude, effectiveness, and content. She entered the Hiroshima Prefecture Speech Contest twice and won first place both times.

Sadako's older brother, Masahiro, entered the same contest and took second place with his speech "Cry for Peace." Masahiro's speech not only appealed for peace but told the story of his sister's death. The contest results were reported in every newspaper and received wide publicity just as the large-scale statue movement was itself making news. Both Noriko's and Masahiro's speeches were aired on the Radio Chugoku and NHK Radio stations.

Having moved to Ushita (a neighborhood in north Hiroshima) in the fourth grade, Noriko Mandai had no personal experience of the atomic bomb tragedy. Nor had she been a classmate of Sadako. She had only participated in the contest at Mr. Matsuura's suggestion. Now, the overwhelming reaction to her speech was causing her problems. When reporters asked her about Sadako or the statue movement, she had no idea what to say. This was considerably upsetting to the serious-minded girl.

The memorial compositions collected through Mr. Matsuura's great effort were compiled into a volume entitled "Kokeshi—For a Certain Star" on July 20. In the process of editing this collection, the group of children known variously as the "former Bamboo class" or "Noboricho Junior High members of the Unity Club" named themselves the "Kokeshi Club." They found that "Kokeshi Club" was how they came to be known in the statue movement. They also found that the Kokeshi Club was seen as a group that would support the statue campaign from the sidelines.

III

On April 1, 1956, the Association for Peace opened an office in the Children's Culture Center in Motomachi and began raising funds in earnest. They had already received 274,345 yen, but it was not nearly enough to build a good statue. They sent out 30,000 prospectuses to schools all over the country.

"Let's build a memorial to the children who perished in the atomic bombing." This plea from the children of Hiroshima had already been sounded nationwide over the radio and in the newspapers. Schools responded swiftly. By August 10, the donations totaled 4,220,627 yen.

But the Association for Peace had an Achilles' heel: the officers were presidents of elementary, junior high, and senior high school student councils, and they turned out to be the main people who showed up for activities. In theory, since all the students at the participating schools were members of the association, any of them could be involved in the activities, but everyone had the impression that it was a group of student council presidents, and so it was.

Part of the rationale must have been that important money matters could not be left up to just anyone. But the main reason that schools only sent their student council presidents was that the teachers believed the organization existed only to raise money for a statue.

As the bylaws show, the group was intended for far more than that. As they worked toward building the monument, they planned to study peace and understand more fully the reality of the bombing—in short, it was to be an organization for a children's peace movement. They were involved in a whole range of activities. They sent representatives to the World Conference against A- and H-bombs. They visited *hibakusha.* They conducted a survey on children who died of atomic bomb illnesses. And although these activities were carried out by only a small group of standing committee members, they were in themselves admirable activities. The problem was that the activities of the association never expanded to include other students from the schools.

Why not? And why could the Association for Peace not have large-scale activities involving all the schools in the city? Beyond the problem of the teachers' perceptions, the organization was composed of students of varying ages from the elementary level to high school, and the structure was inflexible. Standing committee members representing their schools had to be student council presidents. Being a president did not necessarily mean that the student had any particular interest in the bombing. Furthermore, the situation in each school that elected those presidents was quite different.

The students of Noboricho Junior High, the ones who were most cooperative with the association, conducted an interesting survey of themselves around that time. On March 9, 1958, a special edition of the "Noboricho Junior High Newsletter" with the headline " 'Statue for the Children of the A-bomb' to

Be Completed" summarized the activities of the preceding three years. It included the results of a questionnaire distributed to two classes in each grade level, or a total of 365 respondents:

Q: What is the goal of the Children and Students Association for the Creation of Peace?

A: To get children working together to help bring peace to the world—163
No answer—202

Q: Who are the members of this club?

A: Elementary, junior, and senior high student bodies in Hiroshima that support this goal—50
Members of Kokeshi Club—50
Students of Noboricho Junior High—42
Children who love peace—6
Student representatives—7
Ninth graders—6
No answer—185

Q: Are you a member of the Association?

A: Yes—40
No—213
Don't know—112

Q: Around when will the statue be finished?

A: May 5—128
April—27
March—7
Around summer—6
Sometime this year—1
No answer—79

Q: How much money was raised to build this statue?

A: Around 5,000,000 yen—334
No answer—31

Q: How have you participated in this movement?

A: By contribution—5
Signature on petition—5
Saw a play—8
No answer—299

Since these results were obtained in March, two months prior to the completion of the statue, it is not surprising that half of the children knew the date of completion and the amount of money raised. On the other hand, few knew much about the composition of the Association for Peace or had participated in its activities. At that point all fundraising had been completed, perhaps before the new seventh-graders had a chance to contribute. Even given that possibility, it is strange that only 5 of 365 clearly stated that they had donated to the statue.

The writer was a ninth-grader at Kogo Junior High in Hiroshima at the time and still remembers donating to the cause. A special issue of the student council newsletter "Sakae" (No. 6, August 5, 1956) featured the A-bomb and the statue movement. The following is quoted from the front page:

> The movement gained momentum and enlisted the aid of elementary, junor high, and senior high schools to form a "Statue for the Children of the A-bomb" Preparation Committee. *Around October of last year*, they unanimously decided to give the committee the name "Children and Students Association for the *Preservation* of Peace." [emphasis added]

This was the beginning of an informal discussion of the circumstances surrounding the start of the movement. No names are given, but participants in the newsletter discussion were student officers and were probably involved in the movement. Still, there are two clear mistakes in this statement. "Creation" in "Association for the Creation of Peace" was mistakenly changed to "Preservation," and the correct date of formation was January of that year. These mistakes do not appear to be printing errors. They must have been made either by the speaker himself, the one who recorded the discussion, or the editor, all of whom were leading members of the Noboricho Junior High community. Even this so-called leader of the movement had no clear memory of the name of the group or the date it was founded, so the low level of awareness among the general student population probably could not be helped. Despite the idealistic goals of the association and the passionate involvement of its standing committee members, the organization was quite distant from the rest of the students.

The Association for Peace had another Achilles' heel. Neither the standing committee members nor the teachers involved with them had known Sadako Sasaki. From the point of view of the avowed purposes of the association, this should not have made any difference. The statue was to be built for all the children who had perished because of the bombing and was not specifically tied to Sadako. However, even in the prospectus sent to every school in the country, the story of Sadako figured prominently. Anyone reading the prospectus would have assumed that Sadako's classmates were among the leading members of the association.

Incidentally, it was the prospectus that first informed children all around Japan that Sadako folded paper cranes until her death.

Frankly, the Association for Peace felt that the image of Sadako as tragic heroine was necessary to the success of the movement; it is a fact that they made her their star. As the movement expanded, the media also helped make Sadako the main character. Newspaper reporters who appeared at the association office were much more interested in "the young girl who died of leukemia" than in the group's activities. Sadako's death made a good story. However, the main members of the association had never known Sadako; they were forced to involve Sadako's classmates, especially the members of the Kokeshi Club, because they had. As the movement grew, the Kokeshi Club members were pushed time and again into the media spotlight and dragged out for every public event.

Of course, since every student of the participating schools was a member of the Association for Peace, it could be considered natural for the Kokeshi Club members to participate in the activities. The problem was that they were not cooperating as equals. Sadako's classmates were now eighth-graders. And they were very ordinary students, whereas the association was run by student council officers. The Kokeshi Club members were in no position to have opinions about what the association chose to do. But when their presence was necessary, they were herded up and sent to solicit contributions on the street or to appear at lectures.

On April 7 and 8, 1956, the Association for Peace took to the streets to solicit contributions. In addition to the student council presidents from each member school were Principal Tanaka and Mr. Toyota. The Kokeshi Club, who had been asked to participate, stood in the rain along with the others, straining their voices to call to passersby. While the association paid for transportation and lunch for its members, the Kokeshi Club members, who lived nearby, were left completely on their own.

"Asked" is too nice a word. In fact, the Kokeshi Club members were ordered to participate by the teachers who were overseeing their activities. When they grumbled among themselves on the street corner, the teachers said, "You're the ones who started it all, aren't you? If you don't do anything to help, do you think you're doing right by Sadako?" There was no arguing with that.

Probably another factor was that Principal Tanaka, Mr. Toyota, and Mr. Matsuura found it easier to control these students from their own school than to control association officers from other schools. In any case, it was within this climate that Sadako's classmates, particularly those who had gone on to Noboricho and become the Kokeshi Club, came to function as a subordinate subgroup of the association. They were, in effect, an action corps to be used.

Under such circumstance, more and more disgruntled voices

were raised within the Kokeshi Club. Students who had been enthusiastic about building the statue drifted off one by one. The reasons given included increasing involvement in other school clubs and unwillingness to be forced to talk about Sadako on the radio. Also, some were frankly tired of the whole thing.

The monument was completed on May 5, 1958, the year the Kokeshi Club members graduated from junior high. They had spent their entire junior high years on the movement. Including the period that Sadako was in the hospital, they had spent four whole years in constant touch with the A-bomb. When they first talked of a statue in the fall of their seventh grade, they were still like elementary-school children in many ways, but as the movement progressed they grew up in body and mind. It is little wonder that voices of rebellion and suspicion were raised among them. The movement was creating rifts among the Unity Club members.

During the period when the media were spreading news about the statue movement to the entire country and the Kokeshi Club members were appearing on television, radio, and in the newspapers, Nobuhiko Jigo was insulted by a classmate who had gone to a different school.

"Hey Nobu, you've got it great over there," the classmate said. "You get to be on radio, TV, you're a star. But don't forget, you weren't the only ones who wanted to make a statue."

"Of course, I never forget." Nobuhiko, who was, after all, the president of the Unity Club, tried desperately to show his classmate the situation from the point of view of those at Noboricho, but his words had little effect. That the Kokeshi Club had been formed at all was a bit odd.

After that, Nobuhiko's interest in the statue cooled quickly. He often said to the others, "Hey, we're done now, right? Our job is finished. Let's leave the rest to the association maniacs."

Yet they hung on until the statue was finished. Their discontent and resentment at the contradictions in their role did not prevent them from giving everything they had to the project; they felt they had to see it through. They were never interested in issues that were over their heads, like world peace or the abolition of nuclear weapons. They merely wanted to hold to the promise they had made to Sadako when they prayed for the repose of her soul. That was enough.

IV

On July 25, the eighth-graders at Noboricho Junior High who had been Sadako's classmates put out a collection of their writings in rememberance of her; they called the collection "Kokeshi." They started out to make a simple hand-printed booklet, but ended up typesetting it and including respectable gravure photographs. Mr. Matsuura emptied his savings account to cover most of the printing costs. The booklet contained six pages of photographs, a narrative of eighty-nine pages, and a cover design by Shinichiro Hayashi.

The first page read: "We dedicate this collection to the soul of Sadako Sasaki." Photos of Sadako and her family, the Red Cross Hospital, Noboricho Elementary, and recent shots of her classmates followed. The first of the four-part text included compositions and letters by Sadako, a memorial by her family, and contributions by her physician, Dr. Joji Numata, and by one of the nurses, Yoshie Yasunaga.

The second part included compositions and poems by the members of the Kokeshi Club. The third consisted of letters received from all over the country; the fourth contained the two manuscripts from the speech contest mentioned before, and a message from the Kokeshi Club to the schools of the country. Written less than a year after her death, the words came straight from the students' hearts and never fail to move.

You Were Killed by the Devil
By Nobuhiko Jigo

Who killed you?
It was the devil, the atom bomb, its flash.
The hateful, hateful atom bomb.
I will bear your grudge until I die.
Bomb, you had no right
to take the life of an innocent child,
who was my friend.
You were killed by the devil.
The only way to comfort you
is to get atom bombs off this Earth.
Rest easy, we'll do the work for you.
We'll plead to the world to get them off
until peace comes.
We'll never rest until we get the hateful figure
of you, devil, off the earth.
For you, our dead and gone friend.

Maybe this is not fine poetry, but it shows Nobuhiko's desperate search for words to reveal his heart. The other poems likened Sadako's death to the creation of a star, or connected it to their participation in the statue movement. Because Nobuhiko Jigo's rages against the evil that caused Sadako's death, so the writer took the liberty of including it here. It shows that her friends did not merely respond with simple grief and prayerfulness.

The editors of the collection were Shinji Miyasako, Fumio Kumagai, and Kokeshi Club representative Yoshihiro Ooka. Sadako's older brother Masahiro also worked hard on the project.

Now in ninth grade, Masahiro was also an active participant in the Association for Peace. He was an active person who fearlessly entered a speech contest on a teacher's recommendation. But more than that, he could hardly sit by quietly while a number of other children worked on a movement for his sister.

Sadako's death had sparked a movement to build a statue, and her entire family found themselves drawn into its vortex. "The young girl who had died folding paper cranes." "The friends who wanted to build a statue for her." The Sasakis' daughter was rapidly becoming "Hiroshima's Sadako." The Sasakis were no longer merely the family that owned a barbershop, but witnesses to a tragedy. They lived their lives hounded by the media.

And not only by the media. Their presence was requested at every event sponsored by the Association for Peace, and every time they were invited, either Shigeo or Fujiko put in an appearance.

The Sasakis were still in financial straits. They were still shouldering heavy debts and business at the barbershop was bad. The new Motomachi location did not attract as many customers as the Hatchobori shop had. And soon, plans to build a Municipal Baseball Stadium in their neighborhood would force them to move yet again.

For a family struggling just to survive from one day to the next, it cannot have been a pleasure continually to offer hospitality to the media and others related to the movement people. But neither Shigeo nor Fujiko ever betrayed resentment as they met with many different people, telling and retelling the story of Sadako. Deep within them was the feeling, "Our daughter was not the only child who died from the A-bomb, yet people are working toward a statue to memorialize her. If we are careless about their feelings, we will incur divine punishment."

An acquaintance of theirs said that the statue would never have been completed if the Sasakis had not been by nature so accommodating. Perhaps this is an overstatement, but it is a testament to the attitude they took.

For Shigeo, Fujiko, and Masahiro, talking about Sadako was reopening an old wound. They must often have wanted to shout, "Enough is enough! Now leave us alone!" But the world did not permit them to be silent or to forget. For the Sasaki family, this must have been a long, painful period.

On August 5, 1956, the day before the eleventh anniversary of the atomic bombing, a young girl hesitantly opened the glass door of the Sasaki barbershop in Motomachi. When Fujiko saw the tall girl in a uniform from the Kokutaiji Junior High School, her clippers stopped in midair. "Kiyo-san? It's Kiyo-san, isn't it?"

The fair-skinned girl nodded. It was Kiyo Okura, who had battled illness alongside Sadako at the Red Cross Hospital. "I'm sorry I fell out of touch," she said, bowing her head. "I knew about Sadako-san, but . . . I'm sorry I couldn't come to the funeral."

"Well, never mind about that, but Kiyo-san, you're all well now, aren't you? Your sickness is all gone?"

This was the girl who had eaten and slept in the same room with Sadako. Fujiko saw her daughter's image next to the girl in front of her.

After joining her hands in prayer in front of Sadako's mortuary tablet, Kiyo drew a tassle of folded cranes from her handbag. "I folded these for Sada-chan. A thousand cranes."

"The two of you sure did fold those things day in and day out, didn't you? Because you thought folding a thousand might make you well." Fujiko's eyes filled with tears. The tiny cranes Kiyo held were bringing up a stream of sad memories.

Kiyo put a handkerchief to her eyes as well. "I promised Sada-chan something. I told her I'd come see her for sure after I got out. But . . ." She turned to face the picture next to the mortuary tablet. "Sada-chan, I'm sorry."

"Okura-san," said Mr. Sasaki. "Please let us offer up these cranes tomorrow when we go to the Cenotaph. Because Sadako wasn't the only child to die from the bombing. It would make her so much happier for us to do that, than just to display them here," said Mr. Sasaki.

The next day, as promised, the Sasaki family took Kiyo's cranes to the Memorial Cenotaph at the Peace Memorial Park, and made them an offering.

A picture of the Sasaki family holding the cranes in front of the Cenotaph, which was engraved with the words, "Let All The Souls Here Rest In Peace; For We Shall Not Repeat The Evil," appeared in the evening edition of the *Chugoku Shinbun.* The article told about Kiyo Okura as well.

Shortly after that, Ichiro Kawamoto paid a visit to the home of the Okura family in Fujimicho. The person who had thought of the idea of a statue for the children of the A-bomb was still unemployed. Pushed to the sidelines of the movement after the formation of the Association for Peace, he continued to stay in touch with Sadako's classmates, Mr. Matsuura, and Mr. Toyota, and to cooperate with the Association for Peace.

Though he had no voice or role in the group, this unegotistical young man was indifferent to his status or to matters of organization or policy. He was a doer who would go wherever his strength was needed. He participated in the statue movement in his own way, not by making speeches in meetings and debates, but by helping arrange the location and decorating the room. He also prepared the tea cups and made signs for meetings of both the Association for Peace and the Kokeshi Club.

His visit to Kiyo was an example of his special way of bringing people in. A year ago he had invited Sadako's mother to the memorial for Yoshie Iwamoto. Now, after reading the article, he reached out to Kiyo too, and drew her into the movement.

This led directly to Kiyo's joining his Hiroshima *Orizuru Kai,* the Paper Crane Club, in later years. Of course, her motive for joining the club was her relationship with Sadako. Sadako had died, she had lived. How much of her life should be devoted to living in place of Sadako? This question lay heavily in her heart. She had never had much interest in the atom bomb or wars, but Sadako's death started her thinking about these matters.

She felt that Sadako lived in her heart and spoke to her. This was another person whose life had been changed by Sadako's death.

9

Rest in Peace, My Friend

I

By the end of 1956, the contributions received by the Hiroshima Children and Students Association for the Creation of Peace, including interest, had reached 5,395,090 yen. After expenses, there was still 4,770,000 yen left for the statue. To collect this much, within a year of the formation of the Association for Peace, seems miraculous even now. Although adults undeniably smoothed the way, the association could never have raised such funds had not so many children been genuinely enraged about the bombing and wishing from the bottom of their hearts for peace.

In September, the Association for Peace began concrete preparations. It had been informally determined just where in Hiroshima's Peace Memorial Park the statue would stand; now they needed a sculptor and a design.

On September 20, a group of local leaders met to make specific plans for the statue and tried unsuccessfully to choose a sculptor. In the end they requested Mr. Osatake Asano, director of the National Museum, and Mr. Yasuo Kamon, both from Hiroshima Prefecture, to suggest a candidate. On October 10, they received a reply from the two men. Their first choice was sculptor Kazuo Kikuchi, a professor at both Tokyo National University of Fine Arts and Music and Kyoto Art University. The Association for Peace decided on Professor Kikuchi that same day and sent a letter off to him.

On October 15, they submitted a formal application to Mayor Watanabe for a statue in the Peace Memorial Park. Two days later Professor Kikuchi's quick consent arrived in the mail, along with an offer to stop at Hiroshima when he visited Osaka on November 28. With the construction schedule getting settled, the "Statue for the Children of the A-bomb" suddenly took on a new reality.

The one-year anniversary service for Sadako's death was held on October 25, at Shinkoji Temple in Sorozaya-cho. A photograph of the twelve-year-old who had left the world exactly one year ago, a girl whose significance was now beyond anything she herself could have imagined, smiled brightly on the large group in attendance.

At this service, in addition to the friends who knew Sadako in life, were members of the Association for Peace, who had become linked to her after her death. As an offering, they presented their report on the statue movement and some of the messages they had received from all over the country. The Kokeshi Club offered their collection of writings, "Kokeshi."

The sculptor, Kazuo Kikuchi, visited Hiroshima on November 28. Born forty-eight years earlier in 1908, Professor Kikuchi was a member of the Shinseisaku (a group of well-known artists), a recipient of the Mainichi Art Prize, and the author of the book *Rodin.* He stayed at the Yamato Inn (owned by the family of Sadako's classmate Fumiko Yamamoto), and spoke with members of both the Association for Peace and the Kokeshi Club.

After he inspected the statue's projected site and discussed the cost and design with them, he returned home, carrying with him the photograph of Sadako wearing her kimono that Mr. Nomura had taken in the schoolyard after the pregraduation class party.

On January 8, 1957, Hiroshima City formally granted permission for the erection of the statue. In March, Professor Kikuchi visited Hiroshima again, this time carrying a thirty-five–centimeter model of the statue. The plaster model had a girl holding a paper crane over her head, standing on a dome-like pedestal with three legs. Flanking her on the sides of the pedestal were the figures of two dancing children.

The members of both the Association for Peace and the Kokeshi Club must have shared similar feelings as they gazed at this miniature version of the structure that would one day stand nine meters tall. Professor Kikuchi told them the mold would be ready by December 1957. They would have to wait for the following spring for the statue itself. Still, the plaster model was a big step toward the realization of their dreams. Now it was just a matter of waiting for the day when something exactly like it would stand in the Peace Memorial Park.

As the statue neared completion, both the Association for Peace and the Kokeshi Club were thrown into transition. The goal of Sadako's classmates was at hand; they merely ticked off the days. For the Association for Peace, the statue had been the first, but not the only goal. When the fundraising was over at the end of 1956, they tried to turn to the secondary goals set out in their bylaws—to conduct workshops, discussions, and lectures to promote peace; to educate people about peace through publications, surveys, and correspondence; and other necessary matters.

The association put out their first "News of the Association for Peace" (later renamed "Peace") newsletter on March 10, 1957, just when the plans for the statue were taking shape. They intended the newsletter to be a forum for their surveys, to promote correspondence, and to educate children on peace. After a year of working together, friendships were sprouting among the association committee members. Originally sent by their schools only because they happened to be student council officers, the members found their consciousness of peace issues awakened by the year's activities. Today their newsletters and the book written by Mr. Toyota remain as evidence of the sincere enthusiasm with which they conducted their meetings and their many activities.

But their activities, as mentioned earlier, did not attract the student bodies of their respective schools; they remained limited to a small group. This is clear from the 1957 schedule of events (April 1957–March 1958) printed in the June 30 issue of their newsletter:

1. Have officers' get-together.
2. Hold festivals, e.g., *Tanabata* (Star Festival).
3. Participate in lantern-floating ritual at Peace Festival.
4. Send representatives to the World Conference against A- and H-bombs in Tokyo.
5. Visit facilities for unfortunate children.
6. Visit graves of children who died because of the A-bomb.
7. Comfort patients suffering with A-bomb diseases.
8. Exhibit works by children at autumn culture festival.
9. Increase correspondence with children throughout the country.
10. Increase correspondence with children in other countries (e.g., China, the United States, the Soviet Union).
11. Conduct workshops and lectures on peace.
12. Plan Christmas gathering.

These activities were obviously planned for a very small group of students, not the entire student bodies of thirty-eight participating schools. Evidently, none of the events even took place at one of the participating schools.

This is not to accuse the members of idleness. However exclusive their organization was, the standing committee members definitely threw themselves wholeheartedly into what they were doing. While researching this book, the writer learned that the association has been criticized somewhat both then and now. Their newsletters, however, reveal the purity of their search for anything that children could do to bring peace. It must also be remembered that without this group, there would have been no statue. The teachers helping them also must have subjected themselves to extraordinary hardships to carry through these projects. In their own way, the Association for Peace members were as passionate as Sadako's classmates. Unfortunately, the terms for school officers lasted only one year. If they had been able to continue their involvement, their budding interest in peace might have grown and become more deeply rooted in Hiroshima soil.

During this period, the Association for Peace moved its office from the Children's Culture Center to the library office at Noboricho Junior High School. Although the exact date is unclear, by the time the third issue of their newsletter was published on June 30, 1957, the move had been made. A year later in August 1958, after the statue was completed, they moved again, to the YMCA. Since the first move came at the end of fundraising to make construction planning easier, the two moves seem to symbolize the rise and fall of the group.

II

On April 1, 1957, the "Law Pertaining to the Medical Treatment of A-bomb Survivors" (Hibakusha Medical Care Law) was enacted; A-bomb Health Books were issued beginning June 3. During the next thirteen days, 63,000 survivors thronged to the appropriate city offices to get their books; this represents a good indication of their anxiety about their health. The law was based on the recognition that society bears responsibility for A-bomb–related diseases and that the government therefore should bear the cost of treatment. It was hailed as an epoch-making act, but in actuality its provisions fell far short of providing the assistance required.

Even as the statue moved toward completion, the lives of more young children like Sadako were lost. The fourth edition of the association's newsletter carried a survey reporting the names of child residents of Hiroshima who had died of A-bomb diseases. These are the names listed as having died since Sadako's death in October 1955:

Yoshito Kiyomi, age 10, died January 24, 1956

Emiko Hayashi, age 14, died August 9, 1956

Noriyuki Iwata, age 12, died March 30, 1957

Satonori Yamanaka, age 16, died June 19, 1957

There were undoubtedly many others missed by this survey.

Emiko Hayashi was in the eighth grade when she died in August 1956. When she was in seventh grade, she was in my class at Kogo Junior High. When the bomb fell, Emiko was more than four kilometers away from the hypocenter at her home in Furuta-cho. She was always perfectly healthy until the second semester of seventh grade. I remember that she went to the hospital during winter break to have her tonsils removed, and the examination revealed that she had acute myelogenous leukemia. She was quickly transferred to the Red Cross Hospital.

I also remember going to see her at the hospital during the spring of 1956. She had been round-faced, with slightly dark skin. In just two or three months she had become quite pale and was almost unrecognizably wasted away. Her transformation stabbed me in the heart. The slight spasms that sent ripples now and then through her outstretched legs are etched in my memory.

That same fall, an A-bomb Survivors Physical Examination at my school revealed an abnormality in my own blood cell counts. A closer examination showed a slight case of anemia. I have remained healthy, but I remember well how frightened I was after that first examination.

I am sure other *hibakusha* have had similar experiences. When *hibakusha* examinations began on a regular basis, many agonized over them, wondering, "What if . . . ?" Some were so worried about what an exam might reveal that they stubbornly refused to submit to them, or even to apply for an A-bomb Health Book. These fears still lurk inside *hibakusha*; any bodily change immediately draws our anxious attention. This tendency will probably remain throughout our lives.

Members of both the Association for Peace and the Kokeshi Club visited Emiko Hayashi in the hospital. On the first of August, eight days before her death, they were carrying gifts around to cheer up patients at four different hospitals and visited Emiko as well. The impression this experience left on one of the Kokeshi Club members was recorded in the fifth issue (August 5, 1957) of the association's newsletter:

Emiko-san
by the Kokeshi Club

When we went to see you
in the Red Cross Hospital last year,
you were sleeping in a bed
on the hot third floor.

The doctor said
even transfusions
wouldn't help anymore.

Emiko-san,
you were only skin and bones.
Your grandmother fanned you.

Then on August 9
you died.
You died, just like Sadako-san.

We looked for
but couldn't find your house,
and so couldn't pay our respects.

We still feel bad about that.
Emiko-san,
you won't come back anymore.

Emiko Hayashi was the same age as Sadako, but fell ill about a year later. They both had acute leukemia, and they died in the same hospital. Sadako's classmates could not have kept her death distant from them. The poem appeared in the fifth issue of the "Peace" newsletter, along with an announcement about the completion of the model for the statue. Working ahead of his schedule, sculptor Kikuchi had completed a one-quarter-size model by the end of July, and promised to finish the statue by spring.

When Nobuyoshi Tetsumasu, a second-year student at Sanyo High School, and Masahiro Sasaki, now a first-year student at Motomachi High School, represented the Association for Peace at the Third World Conference against A- and H-bombs in Tokyo, they went by to see the one-quarter scale model. They talked about asking nuclear physicist and Nobel Prize laureate Hideki Yukawa to present the Association for Peace with a bell that would hang under the pedestal. Through Mr. Kikuchi's efforts, this idea was confirmed on November 1.

Around the same time, association adviser Kiyoshi Toyota

wrote the lyrics of a song for the Kokeshi Club entitled "For a Certain Star." The tune was written on request by composer Gento Uehara, and the song became a great favorite among the club members. Even after the Association for Peace and Kokeshi Club had faded away, the song continued to be sung by the Hiroshima Orizuru Kai.

On July 27 of that year, the Kyodo Film Company approached the Association for Peace with a production plan for a movie entitled *A Thousand Cranes*. The association decided to participate. *A Thousand Cranes* was released in June 1958. The Hiroshima junior high students who appeared in it would form the nucleus of the Hiroshima Orizuru Kai, the Paper Crane Club.

Joji Moroi, the screenwriter, gathered material energetically until December 1957 and produced a first-draft screenplay on December 21. On March 20, the scenario for the film was rendered as a children's play at the Hiroshima Hotel. The Kokeshi Club members participated enthusiastically in this public performance.

Based on his research, Mr. Moroi told the story of the statue in a four-part serial entitled "Learning from the A-bomb Statue Campaign" that appeared in the magazine *Hiroshima Education*. His report still speaks to us today, and this writer learned a great deal from it.

The film company's interest shows that news of the statue movement had spread all over the country. Apparently, children throughout the country also knew by this time that Sadako had died while folding a thousand cranes. On December 20, near the end of 1957, the magazine *Shojo* (Young Girl) featured an article called "Paper Cranes for Sadako-chan." In response to the article's appeal, 200,000 paper cranes sent from all over the country were brought by child singer Keiko Kondo (who was the same age as Sadako) to the Sasaki home in Nihomachi.

Tomiko Yokota and other Kokeshi Club members were also present for this event.

The family had moved from Motomachi to Nihomachi, but business did not improve at the new location. The Jimmu Boom had leveled off and was followed by a prolonged recession. The Sasaki family's poverty continued amid the darkening economic climate of Japan. In February of that year, when Prime Minister Kishi replaced Prime Minister Ishibashi, he vowed to stamp out the three vices; corruption, poverty, and violence, but . . .

III

On January 15, 1958, Hiroshima's Tenmaya Department Store held a Shinseisaku exhibition that included Kazuo Kikuchi's "Young Girl Holding Up Crane." The somewhat larger than life-sized bronze figure stood with her left foot slightly in front, stretching her arms diagonally upwards, supporting a two-meter-long golden crane.

Kiyo Okura, now a student at Hiroshima Commercial High School, went to see the exhibition with Ichiro Kawamoto and Masahiro Sasaki. When she saw the face of the girl with braided hair hanging in front of her shoulders, she turned impulsively to Masahiro. It definitely looked like Sadako. Sadako's expression was captured on the face of that figure.

"Sasaki-kun . . ."

He nodded without speaking. Then he murmured, "It does look like her, doesn't it. It looks exactly like Sadako before she got sick."

Contributions for an epitaph for the statue had been solicited since the previous year. Saburo Mashimo of Hiroshima University, Koichiro Tanabe of the Hiroshima Literature Society, Masamichi Suzuki of the Board of Education, and Kenzo

Kobayashi of the *Chugoku Shinbun* would make the selection. After considerable debate they chose:

> This Is Our Cry
> This Is Our Prayer
> To Create Peace in the World

On the back of the monument was inscribed:

> To comfort the souls of our brothers and sisters who died because of the A-bomb, and to appeal to the world for peace, the elementary, junior high, and senior high school students of Hiroshima, with the help of friends all over the country, have joined hands and worked together to build this monument.

> May 5, 1958
> The Hiroshima Children
> and Students Association
> for the Creation of Peace

Under the pedestal, on the sides of the hanging bell donated by Dr. Hideki Yukawa was inscribed in his handwriting: "Peace on Earth and in the Heavens" and "A Thousand Paper Cranes."

Nine days later on March 10, Sadako's classmates graduated from junior high school and set off down new paths in high school or in the working world. Their junior high school years started with Sadako's illness and death and ended with the Statue for the Children of the A-bomb. Especially for the forty-one who had gone to Noboricho (three had transferred to other schools along the way), these years seemed to have been lived for the movement.

Just before graduation, the forty-second issue of the Noboricho Junior High Newsletter (March 9, 1958) devoted two or three pages to a special section, entitled "Statue for the Children of the A-bomb to Be Completed," that reflected on the last three years. Association vice-president Junji Asano, adviser Kiyoshi Toyota, and Kokeshi Club member Fumio Kumagai (who was not credited in the article) gave their comments. Fumio's words are interesting:

> I was prouder of being in the Kokeshi Club than in the Association for Peace. Not because I stubbornly wanted to protect our position as the initiators of the movement, but because, as an individual student, I'm more attracted to a small group where you can have an idea and act on it than to a body that's too large to arouse any action at all.

The following account also appeared:

> I don't know when, but sometime when there was some kind of lecture at Hiroshima University, we went out with the student council to get donations on the street. One of my friends said to me on the way, "Hey, this is all we get to do. Do you think it's enough?"
> "Hmmm, I don't know," I answered, shrugging off the question.
> "But really, is this all we can do?" said someone else.

This is a biting criticism of the three-year movement. We can feel the pain in their criticism of the movement that they themselves had ignited. In the midst of reflections and accusations, the Kokeshi Club launched their last activity before the unveiling: They made three huge paper cranes, three meters long each. They carried two of them around to schools in the city. They took the third to a busy street and asked passersby to sign it as a petition calling for the banning of A- and H-bombs. It is unclear who came up with this unconventional idea, but they were busy with their jumbo crane petitioning right up until the day before the unveiling.

Work began in Peace Memorial Park on March 23, 1958. The foundation was underway, and preparations were made to install the statue itself, which would be shipped from Tokyo. The filming of *A Thousand Cranes* began on April 17. Then, on the eve of the unveiling, at 5:30 P.M., May 4, 1958, a reception was held at the Gas Building. This is what a few Kokeshi Club members remembered about that reception:

"I don't know what to say. There were a lot of people I'd never met before."

"That's right. People I'd never seen, who had nothing to do with it, talking like they were something great."

"And they made us guests, see. Lined us up in front, and all these guys who had nothing to do with her saying, 'Sadako this, Sadako that,' just like they knew her. Made me mad."

The gala "Welcome for Our Friends from the Whole Country" was far from a pleasant experience for the Kokeshi Club members. The three-year movement had not followed their desires, but they had put up with it. They had their pride as the originators of the movement. Although it had ballooned out of their control, they had desperately tried to hang onto the fact that they were the seeds.

To make matters worse, something especially disheartening happened that night. They had squeezed time from their busy schedules since junior high graduation to carry out their jumbo crane petition drive. They had hoped to display these cranes at the unveiling the next day, and then planned to send them to the United States, the Soviet Union, and the United Kingdom (the three countries that possessed nuclear weapons at the time) as an appeal for the banning of A- and H-bombs. The cranes were made of construction paper, and the trip around to different schools and the petition drive had dirtied and crumpled them. The children tried to smooth out the crinkles and repair the tears before they brought them to the reception. But because of some mix-up that is still not clear, the cranes were not presented to the gathering, and worse, they ended up tossed in a corner in a pile of rubbish. Perhaps the cranes were so dirty that someone mistook them for trash.

True, the cranes were not particularly attractive, but how would the thousands of people who signed their names feel? Silently, Sadako's classmates picked up their totally crumpled cranes and set off for home. Association adviser Mr. Toyota, however, adamantly denies that this happened. He remembers the atmosphere of the reception as friendly. He has no memory of the children bringing jumbo cranes with signatures either to the reception or to the unveiling.

IV

Until the 1960s, greenery was quite scarce in Hiroshima. The city looked flat and was always covered in dust. Everything was stark and bright. Hiroshima city was filled with hasty, postwar architecture dominated by low, two-story buildings. The transplanted trees in the green zones were still saplings with no leafy branches. There were wide roads, like Hundred Meter Road, Fifty Meter Road, and MacArthur Road, but without buildings and trees to provide shade, the impression was of sun and empty blue sky. Today, Peace Memorial Park is so covered with trees we could call it wooded, but when the Statue for the Children of the A-bomb was built, the only other structures to catch the eye in the wide, bare space were the concrete Peace Memorial Museum and the City Auditorium.

The spot chosen for the statue was a green area in the northeast part of the park, close to the bank of the Motoyasu River. It was just across the river from the A-bomb Dome and, turning around, one could see the Cenotaph with the Peace Memorial Museum beyond.

The unveiling was held on May 5 at 10:00 A.M. One hundred and thirty elementary, junior high, and senior high school students from all over Hiroshima and elsewhere in Japan came to the event. There as special guests were sculptor Kazuo Kikuchi and Takeo Haniu, principal of Nishi Ashibetsu Junior High School in Hokkaido, who had helped the movement since the beginning. In all, five hundred people came to the unveiling.

First, Association for Peace president Nobuyoshi Tetsumasu gave a report on the movement. Contributions so far totaled 5,800,000 yen; 3,550,000 of that had gone to the sculptor. The rest had gone to construct the foundation and to other campaign expenses. Sculptor Kikuchi gave an address and the inscriptions were read aloud. Then, Sadako's brother Eiji and sister Mitsue unveiled the statue. Mitsue, ten when Sadako died, was now twelve, as old as her sister had been when she died. As the white curtain covering half the monument dropped away, a slender six-meter steeple-shaped pedestal appeared, and on it, a bronze statue of a young girl holding over her head a folded crane made of gunmetal. The crane and the life-sized figure together were about three meters tall. The whole monument soared nine meters into the blue May sky. This symbol of a young life facing the future with wings in full flight against the sparse trees in the background struck the gathering powerfully. After a commotion of whispered oohs and aahs died down, the crowd broke into thunderous applause. Forgetting everything, Sadako's classmates, too, clapped with all their might. Three years of trouble had ended in a thing of beauty.

After the unveiling, it was time for Kokeshi Club member Fumio Kumagai to ring the bell hanging under the pedestal. Fumio was now in his first year at Motomachi High School. His family had run a cosmetics store in Horikawa-cho, but both of his parents were killed by the A-bomb. Fumio and his brother escaped injury because they had been evacuated previously to the suburbs. Their home was reduced to ashes. Their entire family was wiped out. They never knew what became of their mother. Their father clung to life until the end of August and then died of A-bomb disease. Fumio and his brother were raised by their grandmother, their only surviving relative in the city.

Fumio has a faint memory of wandering through the burnt ruins looking for his mother in mid-August. He vaguely remembers walking along cheerfully, as if he were on a picnic, too young to understand death. After the war his great uncle tried to rebuild the family business but quickly went bankrupt and lost the family's property. Fumio's life had been such that no amount of hating the bomb could be enough. These three years he had been totally absorbed in working to build the statue.

Now, he stood alone under the pedestal. Before him a chain dangled from a flat metal ringer in the bronze bell high over his head. A metal crane hung from the midpoint of this chain. Fumio pulled down hard. *Dong.* The peal of the bell was too light. He pulled again, but something unexpected happened. The flat ringer was stuck in one end of the oval bell. Frantically, Fumio jerked the chain two or three more times, but the bell, five meters above him, only shook.

None of the onlookers knew what was going on. Puzzled faces greeted him as he descended from the platform after just one small ring. From that time on, Fumio was of the opinion that both bells and ringers should be round.

Next, guests made congratulatory remarks until the ceremony ended just after noon. When the crowd dispersed and quiet returned to the park, the Kokeshi Club members gathered in a corner to burn their jumbo cranes. Three meters from wingtip to wingtip, the birds were a mass of tears and crinkles.

"It's over, isn't it," Naohiko Jigo muttered, staring into the flames.

"It really is. It's over." Atsuko Nomura turned toward the statue. "We did good, didn't we."

"I wonder if we really wanted to put up something like that?" Hiromi Sorada cocked her head doubtfully to one side.

They fell into silence. Their joy in the completion of the statue was accompanied by a wordless emptiness.

"In any case, it's over! The whole thing!" Nobuhiko Jigo's tone was almost a shout. "OK, then. I've got practice after lunch.

We gotta go home. Hey Nao, let's go." He called in irritation to his older twin and set off quickly. Behind Nobuhiko's broad back the golden crane glittered in the May sunlight atop the Statue for the Children of the A-bomb.

As of this date the Kokeshi Club ceased to exist. Not one of them participated in any of the other association activities. The effort of the last three years had not left them with pleasant memories. "Did we want to put up such a huge statue? In the end, weren't we manipulated by adults toward their own ends?"

Their self-scorn has grown over the subsequent thirty years and still lies heavily in their hearts. They were driven to these feelings by a variety of forces. The media continued to harass them even after the statue's completion. Even more disturbing, one of their members died three months after the unveiling, and this may also have contributed to their determination to refuse all comment about the movement. "Enough is enough!"

Constant questioning about Sadako and the statue movement, even in later years, has given them all mild to severe allergies to the Statue for the Children of the A-bomb.

But as the Kokeshi Club died, the Unity Club was reborn. The Kokeshi Club had been a temporary thing without the claim on their hearts of the Unity Club. With their sixth-grade teacher Tsuyoshi Nomura as nucleus, the Unity Club weathered the storm of the statue movement and continues to meet now, more than thirty years later. Even Ken Hosokawa, who had responded so negatively to the statue movement, feels comfortable at Unity Club meetings, sometimes sharing his memories of Sadako. The now forty-year-old Unity Club members do not consider the statue either a plea for peace or a memorial to the children who died from the A-bomb. It is, for them, simply a statue of Sadako Sasaki, an expression of their pain at the loss of a dear classmate. This, at any rate, is what they want to believe.

10

A Genealogy of
Paper Cranes

I

On June 21, 1958, about two months after the unveiling, there was a special preview of the just-completed film *A Thousand Cranes* at the theater in the Fukuya Department Store. Sadako's classmates, the Association for Peace, and others related to the film were invited to another preview the following day.

The film was jointly produced by the Kyodo Film Company and the Association for Peace and was just over an hour long. Seventy Hiroshima junior high students appeared in it, along with members of a Tokyo children's theater company. The film was shot entirely on location. The director was Sotoji Kimura, the screenwriter, Joji Moroi. Following the facts for the most part, *A Thousand Cranes* depicted the death of Sadako (whose name was written with slightly different characters), the leafletting by the students of Mr. Nomura (Mr. Kitagawa in the film) at the principals' conference, and the activities of the Association for Peace. The newly erected Statue for the Children of the A-bomb appeared in the last shot.

On June 22, the day of the second and last preview, the people involved in building the statue and the junior high students who appeared in the film held a party to thank director Kimura, screenwriter Moroi, and the rest of the production staff in a classroom of the Hiroshima YMCA in Motomachi. During this party someone said it would be a shame if this group that had just gotten together should fall apart right away. He suggested forming an organization to study peace issues and perpetually conduct related activities. The motion carried unanimously. The group born that day was the Hiroshima Orizuru Kai, the Paper Crane Club; the suggestion came from Ichiro Kawamoto.

According to the records, members of a children's theater company in Tokyo also formed a Tokyo Orizuru Kai at this time. A newspaper article reporting the Hiroshima Orizuru Kai meeting on August 6 of that year also mentioned a Shimane Orizuru Kai. We can infer that people in various places responded to the Hiroshima group's call to form Orizuru Kais. Since no record exists of any of their activities, these groups probably faded out of existence before too long. The sole exception was the Kodama no Kai, the Echo Club, in Kure. The children who formed the Kodama no Kai enthusiastically developed it in line with the activities of the original group and kept it alive even after a move to Fukuyama.

The newly formed Hiroshima Orizuru Kai moved into action immediately. The first thing they did was fold cranes for the Fukuya Movie Theater and patients at the Hiroshima Atomic Bomb Hospital. This plunge into activities even before the structure of the group had been laid down was a sure sign of the influence of Mr. Kawamoto.

The Orizuru Kai finally held its first organizational meeting at the YMCA on June 29, and chose Takeshi Kabuto of Kokutaiji Junior High and Ryuichi Otsubo of Noboricho Junior High as representatives. The club was made up originally of students who had appeared in the film, but by this time others had joined. Sadako's older brother Masahiro, of Motomachi High School, Kiyo Okura, of Hiroshima Commercial High School, and other high school students connected to Sadako joined at Mr. Kawamoto's invitation, raising the membership to over sixty. Mr. Matsuura, who had been adviser to the Kokeshi Club, evidently helped Mr. Kawamoto in guiding the club.

It is sad somehow that Sadako's classmates, who had been so impassioned about the statue, stayed away from this new organization. Because of the course taken by the movement they had set in motion, they broke with it at this point. For Mr. Kawamoto, however, that day in November 1955 when he had first suggested a statue had led straight down this particular road; the movement he had envisioned was still on track. From the leafletting to the completion of the statue, this young man had supported hidden elements of the movement, making his own efforts out of his personal attachment to the statue. He was determined not to let the completion of the statue end the children's movement. This new group would make up for the weaknesses of the old. This time, Mr. Kawamoto was eager to create an ideal organization.

Like others, he had learned many lessons during the course of the three-and-a-half-year movement. One was that any organization too closely connected with the student council activities of a certain school was surprisingly vulnerable. Another was that whenever a group that exists purely to work for peace begins to take on an air of ideology or politics, it instantly comes under pressure and is crushed.

Therefore, Mr. Kawamoto determined that members of the Orizuru Kai must participate freely, as individuals. They would meet at the YMCA or at his house, never at a school facility.

From year to year, club members would be associated predominantly with certain schools, but he was always careful to draw a clear line between school life and the club.

He was extremely skittish about any political activity on the part of club members. If any group that wanted contact with them smelled at all of political affiliation, he instantly turned them away. Furthermore, he did not tolerate individual relationships or dating between boys and girls within the club, a precaution to forestall accusations that the club was a potential hot-bed for unhealthy activity. Mr. Kawamoto's values created a rather strained atmosphere that naturally fostered resistance among club members.

For one thing, the black-and-white sense of justice that is characteristic of youth tends to make them politically impetuous. For another, because war itself is an extremely political act, any organization that opposes it unavoidably takes on a political atmosphere. Ironically, so-called nonpolitical, nonideological peace movements often have quite a strong political air, as we see in peace groups around us today. Mr. Kawamoto had chosen a difficult path for the Orizuru Kai.

"Just folding cranes and giving them to *hibakusha* is supposed to make peace?"

"Clean up around the statue? That's our activity?"

"Is praying going to get rid of nuclear weapons?"

"We want you to give us more credit. If we discuss things and make our own decisions about activities, we don't like you ordering us around about them."

After all, these were students who had joined because of their intense interest in peace or the A-bomb; their repulsion from the club was strong and sharp. The more than sixty members who had joined at the outset dwindled day by day, until membership settled at around twenty.

And yet, among those who remained were some who began to

appear almost every day at Mr. Kawamoto's house—"shack" is more accurate—near the A-bomb Dome, even eating meals together.

Kiyo Okura related these memories:

> How can I explain? It was like we were part of his family, spending most of our time at his house. We called Mr. Kawamoto *"Onii-san*—Big Brother." If he had an idea, we'd all jump in and work on it. It was fun. But looking back on it, it never occurred to us that he might have needed more privacy than we gave him. We were just kids and didn't think of adults as individuals with lives to live. We thought nothing of staying at his house until really late at night.

Thus, Kiyo's account reveals that the Orizuru Kai at that time carried out activities in a family-like atmosphere, with Mr. Kawamoto's home as nucleus. It is not true that the club was limited to visiting *hibakusha*, folding cranes, and cleaning up around the statue. They were involved in all sorts of activities. On one occasion, a bicycle relay linking Nagasaki, Hiroshima, and Tokyo was held before the Fourth World Conference against A- and H-bombs. When the cyclists passed through Hiroshima on July 26, the Orizuru Kai accompanied them as far as Kure, handing them messages for the peoples of France, Switzerland, and West Germany, as well as for people in Japan. The messages included the information that Orizuru Kais were forming in Tokyo, Nagoya, and Hokkaido, and that Tokyo's Toshima Ward had distributed 100,000 pieces of origami to children for making paper cranes. This let people know that the movement to fold paper cranes for peace was spreading nationwide.

On another occasion, they took a circus chimpanzee into the Atomic Bomb Hospital. On another they obtained permission to hold a New Year's Fire Brigade Parade near the hospital for the enjoyment of patients. According to a newspaper article, a memorial service attended by two thousand children was held in front of the statue on August 6, sponsored jointly by the Orizuru Kai, the YMCA Youth Division, and the Association for Peace.

The preceding day (August 5), an article in the *Chugoku Shinbun* reported that on August 3 the family of Sadako Sasaki changed residence from Nihomachi to Wakakusacho and opened shop there. It noted that Mr. Matsuura and the Orizuru Kai were on hand at the opening to wish the new shop well.

Mr. Sasaki's health had been deteriorating since the move in the spring of 1957 from Motomachi to Nihomachi, and by now he had been driven to bed. The family's grinding poverty and Sadako's death had worn his body and soul to tatters. After the completion of the statue, and while the film *A Thousand Cranes* was being shown, a rumor began going around that the Sasaki family had received considerable money in donations and model fees. Bill collectors heard the rumor and thronged to Mr. Sasaki's bedside.

Nothing could have been further from the truth. The Sasakis never received any money from either the statue project or the film. If anything, being pulled here and there for various events and chased by the media hindered the family business. It was certainly no "plus." If all this had happened anywhere but Hiroshima, the "family of Sadako" might have enjoyed increased business from the connection. But in Hiroshima many other families had lost children to the atomic bombing. Sadly, not all of them welcomed the idea of Sadako becoming nationally famous as "Hiroshima's young girl."

"The Sasakis were not the only ones who lost a daughter to the bombing. Our daughter died a much crueler death." There were definitely some with this attitude, and in the presence of their cold stares the Sasakis had to keep their eyes cast humbly down.

After opening the new shop in Wakakusacho, Shigeo Sasaki

forced his recuperating body to pick up the clippers once again. But business was poor. Although reporters were no longer pushing their way through the door every day, there was no erasing their public image as the bereaved family of "Hiroshima's young girl, Sadako."

II

The Orizuru Kai had formed after a preview showing of the film *A Thousand Cranes*. As they were carrying out their own special activities and building their record of achievements, what path was the Association for Peace following? The exact date of the group's end has not been confirmed, but it is clear that the Association for Peace still existed in January 1959. In a sense, the history of the association after the unveiling in May 1958 is tragic.

Sometime during the period between the unveiling and July of the same year, they moved their office from the library of Noboricho Junior High to a room in the Boys' Division of the YMCA in Motomachi. None of the people involved who were interviewed for this book knew the reason for that move. One possibility may have been pressure from those who felt it was inappropriate for the association to maintain an office in a public school. In other words, now that the statue was completed, supporting the group was no longer considered necessary; to continue could be considered pushing the students toward political activism. This misgiving seemed to be held by both school authorities and the city government. Another reason was that after the statue was finished, enthusiasm for the group cooled rapidly within the student councils of the participating schools.

The yearly turnover of the standing committee members of the association meant that none of the members by that time had known the organization at its beginning. They may not have felt very strongly attached to it. On July 4, two months after the statue was completed, association president Nobuyoshi Tetsumasu and some standing committee members made leaflets at their new office in the YMCA, urging all members to gather under the statue on August 6, but only a few actually showed up. One hundred children and students had attended each of their annual meetings prior to the unveiling, and five hundred people came to the unveiling itself. Why such a decline less than three months later? There are no clear reasons, but some information about the history of peace education in Hiroshima might be helpful.

When the term "peace education" came into use has not been established. It certainly did not exist during the early postwar period, possibly because it did not seem necessary. The new Japanese constitution instituted peace and democracy as its most important principles. Education was expected to fall in line. In other words, in the early postwar period, all education was peace education. Then, when the allied occupation made a dramatic policy turnabout and Japan found itself rearming, postwar education changed its nature as well.

Still, passages opposing war were common in 1950s textbooks. For example, in 1950 a section chief in the Ministry of Education suggested that seventh-grade social studies classes study the devastation of war as follows:

1. Students study problems in their daily lives that have been affected by the war.
2. Classes discuss how these problems can be resolved.
3. Students report in class on those who still suffer from the war, including orphans, repatriots, and evacuees.

In October 1951 Mr. Arata Osada compiled a collection of memories of children who had suffered the bombing, a book he entitled *Genbaku no Ko* (Children of the A-bomb). During the following year, children who had contributed to this collection formed a group called the Fellowship Association of A-bomb Children, surely the first group of children to gather to discuss their experiences in the bombing.

But before parents and teachers could integrate into school curricula the means for children to learn from the experiences of *hibakusha*, a conservative swing took over in education. In 1955 the Democratic Party (the present Liberal Democratic Party) issued a pamphlet called "The Distressing Problem of Our School Textbooks," and two laws that stipulated the neutrality of education were forcibly passed. It was becoming increasingly difficult to plead the cause of peace within the education system.

In 1956 the system of publicly electing members of Boards of Education was abolished. The following year the Ehime Prefecture Board of Education initiated efficiency ratings for teachers; this spread to the entire country by 1958. This rating system was seen by many as merely a way for the government to have tighter control over the teachers. Soon the so-called "union campaign against efficiency ratings" was springing up everywhere. The first signs of the chasm growing between teachers and principals in Hiroshima schools became visible during this period. It was as this trend was developing that the statue was completed and the Association for Peace, as an organization composed of representatives from various city schools, was terminated.

Also in 1958, all mention of the atomic bombing was erased from elementary social studies textbooks. Pictures of the mushroom cloud over the ruined city of Hiroshima were replaced by pictures of the restored city and of Hideki Tojo, Chief of General Staff and Prime Minister during World War II. That the Association for Peace, now without school support, could continue any activities until January 1959 testifies to the dedication of Chairman Nobuyoshi Tetsumasu and a few other standing committee members. These individuals continued the association's activities because they had learned something in the process of working toward the statue and wanted to share what they had learned with the students who would come after them.

The tenth and last issue of the association's newsletter "Peace," on January 10, 1959, contains a sad plea:

Let's Make May 5 "Thousand Crane Day" for the Children of Hiroshima

Because of our efforts, no, because of Sadako-chan's hope, the paper crane has now become a symbol of peace. The Council against A- and H-bombs [*sic*] is even using a paper crane pin for its campaign to raise relief funds.

As we face the future, our biggest worry is the question of how long we can maintain our sense of unity. After we graduate, will the children and students of Hiroshima support and keep this organization going? It appears that awareness of our group is gradually fading.

In a way this seems unavoidable. We have our schoolwork. The number of *hibakusha* is declining and maintaining the group is too much effort. But since we have worked hard shaping this organization for the last four years, we want like-minded children and students coming after us to protect what we have created. They don't have to make a big splash, as long as they meet every week and seriously think as students about peace.

If the children of Hiroshima don't think about peace, who will? Creating peace is a duty for the children of Hiroshima.

Since the statue was unveiled on May 5, shouldn't there be some appropriate annual remembrance and prayer on that day in front of the statue? I appeal to the children and students of Hiroshima as well as the principals.

By T.

Is "T." the initial of association chairman Tetsumasu? Or is it of adviser Kiyoshi Toyota?

After this newsletter, the name "Association for Peace" ceased to appear in newspaper articles or pamphlets regarding peace events.

One year later in May 1960, two years and ten days after the unveiling, on the morning of the fifteenth, the family of Sadako Sasaki, whom we have to recognize as the source of the movement, was leaving Hiroshima on a train. The family business having failed again at Wakakusacho, they decided to move to Hakata in Kyushu and depend on help from a relative. Since they had no shop in Hakata, Shigeo and Fujiko Sasaki would have to work as mere employees. Masahiro had gone off to hairdresser school in Osaka and Eiji had been adopted by a relative. Sadly, the family had been reduced to the parents and their second daughter, Mitsue.

Some relatives stood on the platform next to the Sasakis' train at Hiroshima Station. They had little to say. The only people related to the statue movement who came to see the Sasakis off were Kiyo Okura and the Orizuru Kai, who had hastened there with their perpetually smiling leader, Ichiro Kawamoto. Before long, the train began to move.

"We'll take care of Sada-chan, of the statue, just leave it to us!" the young man shouted, creasing his suntanned face.

Without speaking, Mr. and Mrs. Sasaki bowed deeply toward the group through the window.

The train slowly picked up speed. The short distance to Yokogawa Station was on an elevated track, so they could look out over the city. Seen from this new perspective, the city was quite beautiful. The Teppocho area where they had once had a shop was now lined with tall buildings. They could barely make out the bell tower of the Nagarekawa Church. Only the area between the Aioi and Misasa Bridges was still a clutter of huts that seemed to cling to the embankment. In 1963, a city councilman referred to this area as the "atomic slum," and that is how it was known ever since.

When would they see these scenes again? Would they ever?

"Look, Shigeo, Sadako is seeing us off!" shouted Fujiko, suddenly rising halfway and pointing toward the Peace Park. For a brief instant they could just see the park across the city, its wooded areas having filled out well over the past two years. Then the train began to run along lower ground and the view was obstructed by passing houses.

"She really did, didn't she?" Shigeo spoke softly to himself. "She saw us off. We've got to be strong, don't we?"

Kyushu was still several hundred kilometers away.

III

While Sadako's family was leaving Hiroshima in despair, the Orizuru Kai members were turning their enthusiam toward another activity. Since its formation, in the midst of all their troubles, they had applied themselves faithfully to their activities. At one point in the past Fumio Kumagai had said this about the statue movement: "I'm much more attracted to a small group where you can have an idea and act on it than to a body that's too large to arouse any action at all." In that sense, the Orizuru Kai came close to Fumio's ideal. In the two years since the statue's completion, the Orizuru Kai had done a number of things. Every year they held a memorial service in front of the statue on the anniversary of Sadako's death, and they always gathered on the anniversary of the unveiling. Their participation in the peace movement included attending peace marches and soliciting signatures on petitions protesting nuclear weapon testing by France. But their daily activities were mainly services like visiting patients with A-bomb–related diseases and keeping the area around the statue clean.

From around August of the year of the unveiling, an enormous number of folded cranes began to appear draped under the statue. Cranes still hang there today in great profusion, and even now, it is the Orizuru Kai that burns the old cranes. Burning a crane that someone went to the trouble to fold and send is painful. The Orizuru Kai exchanges new cranes for old at night, so no one else will have to see the distressing act.

Another important activity of the Orizuru Kai is greeting peace activists from Japan and overseas when they visit Hiroshima. They have met Betty Jean Lifton, the writer, and her husband Robert Jay Lifton, Austrian writer Robert Junk, Barbara Reynolds and her husband from the United States, Professor Brunner of Pacific University, and Honolulu Mayor Blaisdell. They present these foreign visitors with leis of paper cranes and organize welcome gatherings.

They have been variously criticized for these activities.

"You're going to make peace by folding cranes?"

"Isn't wrapping yourselves around foreign dignitaries simply self-advertisement?"

These sorts of critisisms are often counterreactions to the club's posture of extreme aversion to political affiliations. It is certainly unlikely that folding cranes alone will bring about peace, but folding them is better than not folding them. "A thousand paper cranes" has now long been a symbol of peace, but it was Sadako's thousand cranes that created this symbol. The appeals of the Unity Club, Kokeshi Club, and Association for Peace spread the idea, and the Orizuru Kai developed it further. The association of Japan's ancient art of folding paper with the peace movement is a wonderful legacy of the statue movement.

The average Japanese child knows how to fold a crane. Even knowing nothing of the atomic bomb, a child can fold a crane and empathize with Sadako. While gathering material for this book, the writer tried folding a thousand cranes. One thousand is a large number, but if one is determined, it is not a difficult struggle. The best thing about it is that it is simple, manual work. We must use our minds to think about peace, of course, but steadfastly moving our fingers for peace is useful as well. More than hearing or reading the story of Sadako, would not folding a thousand cranes for her leave a lasting memory?

The Orizuru Kai is a genuine force for peace. Thirty years later they continue their watch over the statue, and regularly take down half-ton bundles of old cranes. They also visit *hibakusha* patients. If you ask them, they will tell you that presenting leis of cranes to guests from far away and singing songs for them is no more than a natural welcome.

In 1960, when the revision of the U.S.-Japan Security Treaty enveloped the country in a whirlwind of antitreaty protests, the Orizuru Kai was beginning a new project, the "A-bomb Dome Preservation Movement." Hiroko Kajiyama, a sixteen-year-old student who died of leukemia on April 15, had written in her diary, "Please hand the dome down to future generations so Hiroshima will never be repeated." Struck to the heart by those words, club members began to collect donations and signatures toward the preservation of the dome.

Fifteen years after the bombing, the dome was deteriorating to such an extent that the city government was beginning to believe that it would have to be demolished. Fortunately, the city decided to preserve it in 1964 and repair work began. During that interval, many groups offered contributions and petition signatures. The Orizuru Kai did not collect all of these, but they unquestionably were the spark that ignited the fire.

When the dome was safely preserved, nearly ten years had already passed since Sadako's death in 1955. Now, twenty years after that, the junior high students of the Orizuru Kai still put on their club armbands and work hard on their activities in the city of Hiroshima. Among them are many whose mothers are the same age Sadako would have been. Ichiro Kawamoto, once the "*Onii-san*" of the group, is now over fifty, with many wrinkles lining his sun-weathered face.

The trees in Peace Memorial Park have matured, and the Statue for the Children of the A-bomb, which once shot up into the blue sky, now stands more modestly, overshadowed by tall trees. But under its pedestal, the millions of cranes offered end-lessly, year after year, bear witness that even now something about this statue continues to appeal to children.

Author's Note

It has already been twenty-six years since the Statue for the Children of the A-bomb was erected in Hiroshima's Peace Memorial Park. I was a high school student in Hiroshima at the time and recorded the May 5 unveiling in excited tones in my diary. I was moved by the completion of that statue as a child of Hiroshima, and that feeling remains unchanged to this day, even after writing this book. In fact, listening to the bereaved family of Sadako Sasaki and the many others who were involved in building the statue, my appreciation has deepened.

I believe the Statue for the Children of the A-bomb was destined to be built. If this book communicates even a little of the fervent drive of the boys and girls who felt impelled to build it, and those who supported them, I will be overjoyed.

According to my notes, I started collecting material on June 28, 1982. That means it took two entire years to complete and publish the book. Predictably, the A-bomb was a monstrous, formidable subject to tackle. I could not have finished the work without the warm encouragement of Nobuhiko Jigo, Tomiko Kawano, and others who had been my classmates at Motomachi High School. Ichiro Kawamoto was a great support to me as well.

As I set out to depict the atomic bombing of Hiroshima, I was forced to confront my ignorance. I had experienced the A-bomb when I was three and had lived in Hiroshima for over thirty years, so the bombing was certainly not an unfamiliar subject. But when I actually put pen to paper, I was confronted by question after question; for days I could not write a single line. I then realized that words we use so casually every day, like "*hiba-kusha*" and "A-bomb disease," have their respective histories and special meanings. I have tried in this book to use such terms as accurately as possible.

The descriptions of the horrifying scenes right after the bombing are based primarily on the recollections of Sadako's parents, Shigeo and Fujiko Sasaki; but I also relied heavily on the five-volume book *A-bomb: A City Tells Its Story*, which was compiled by the City of Hiroshima. Parts of my own parents' experiences also appear in places. The *tanka* poems quoted in the story were written by my deceased father, Shigeyoshi Nasu.

Because factual descriptions of conditions on August 6 vary even to this day, I selected data according to my own best judgment. For instance, the explosion time was taken from the U.S. War Plane Flight Diary, and the estimates of the number of dead from *Hiroshima and Nagasaki: The Physical, Medical, and Social Effects of the Atomic Bombings*, compiled by the Committee for the Compilation of Materials on Damage Caused by the Atomic Bombs in Hiroshima and Nagasaki. Since the amount of radiation emitted by the explosion is under debate at this time, I would like to note that I took the figures in this book from "1965 Tentative Dose (T65D)," put out by the United States Oakridge Research Center.

I will also add that the ABCC described in the story was abolished in 1975. Its work has been carried on by a U.S.-Japan joint project called the "Radiation Effects Research Foundation."

I often encountered contradictory memories as I elicited various people's recollections and was forced to choose which version to describe. When I had no basis for judgment, I set down the differing recollections in parallel, for which I ask the reader's understanding.

It was my great privilege to hear valuable anecdotes from many people. Sadako's parents, Shigeo and Fujiko Sasaki, and her brother Masahiro were my most important sources. (The family is currently operating a barbershop in Fukuoka Prefecture and leading a peaceful life.) Tsuyoshi Nomura, the teacher of the Bamboos, was also very helpful.

Sadako's doctor Joji Numata allowed me to read his notes detailing the progress of her disease and the treatment. I also consulted him several times about the nature of leukemia.

Kiyo Okura, who associated very closely with Sadako in the hospital and later became a member of the Orizuru Kai, never failed to answer in thorough detail whenever I phoned or mailed questions to her.

Yukio Matsuura, who supported Sadako's classmates at Noboricho Junior High, was supportive of me as well. Kiyoshi Toyota, faculty adviser to the Association for Peace, who put his heart and soul into the building of the monument, generously made available to me most of the documents related to the association and to Noboricho Junior High at the time. I also quoted from his book, *Habatake Senbazuru*. I also received a great deal of assistance from Ichiro Kawamoto, who first advocated the building of the statue and who still manages the Orizuru Kai.

I also express my warmest thanks to the following members of the Unity Club: Shinji Miyasako, Ken Hosokawa, Shinichiro Hayashi, Toshio Yasui, Nobuhiko Jigo, Fumio Kumagai, Kimiya Haguma, Hiromi Sorada, Hiroko Sasaki, Tomiko Kawano, Masako Sasaki, and Fumiko Takahashi. Not only did I ask them for information, I shamelessly requested their critiques of the writing itself and even asked them to check the proof sheets after the manuscript was completed. They read carefully and pointed out many mistakes.

Others who helped me gather information were: Noriko Ishikawa, who took part in the speech contest during her Noboricho Junior High days; Mariko Asai of the Chugoku Broadcasting Co., who also graduated from Noboricho Junior High and helped me contact Sadako's classmates; and Tetsuro Tsuchiya, who was teaching seventh grade there at the time.

Dr. Shiro Okamoto of Shimane Medical University was my primary source of information about radiation. Akiko Nakamura of the *Chugoku Shinbun* collected relevant articles from that time. Kazuhiko Okamoto helped me obtain photographs from the *Chugoku Shinbun*. Novelist Naoshiro Yoshimoto helped me in many ways while I was collecting material in Hiroshima. Novelist Taichi Kato found the essay by Principal Haniu that appeared in the *Hokkaido Shinbun*. I want to express my gratitude to all of these people.

And also, the people of the Hiroshima Municipal Library, Noboricho Junior High School, and Hiroshima Prefectural Teachers Union who were so cooperative while I was collecting material. Thank you very much.

After finishing this work, I did regret that I could not include much about the activities of the Hiroshima Orizuru Kai. I hope someday to write in detail about the more-than-twenty-year history of this club.

June 1984
Masamoto Nasu

About the Author

Masamoto Nasu was born in 1942 in Hiroshima and graduated from Shimane Agricultural College in 1965. Since 1972 he has written over one hundred books for children, many of which are recommended by the National School Library Council.

Mr. Nasu is best known for his Zukkoke stories. "Zukkoke" is a slang word meaning something like "zany," and the stories are a still-growing series of twenty-two books (as of December 1990) about three adventurous, good-hearted, bumbling boys. Since the publication of *The Go Get 'em Zukkoke Trio* in 1978 (the first volume), titles in the series have been best-sellers. These include *The Zukkoke Detectives, The Zukkoke Trio Travels in Time,* and *The Intrepid Zukkoke Reporters.*

Children of the Paper Crane represents a significant departure from the light-hearted fiction that characterizes the rest of Nasu's work. The Japanese original has sold over twenty thousand copies since its publication in July 1984.

Masamoto Nasu presently lives in Hofu City in Yamaguchi Prefecture with his artist wife and their four children.

About the Translators

Elizabeth Baldwin grew up in Japan and graduated from the University of Wisconsin in 1971. She received a master's degree in social work from Atlanta University in 1982. Ms. Baldwin has worked as a counselor and teacher but has been translating professionally since 1985. She and her husband, Steven Leeper, presently live in Atlanta with their two sons.

Steven Leeper spent six years of his childhood in Japan and received a B.A. from Florida Presbyterian College in 1969 and a master's degree in psychology from West Georgia College in 1978. Mr. Leeper is presently a managing partner of the Transnational Resource Network, a translation and intercultural relations consulting company with offices in Hiroshima and Atlanta.

Kyoko Yoshida graduated in 1983 from Midland Lutheran College in Fremont, Nebraska, with a degree in communication arts. Frequent work in Hiroshima as an interpreter has enabled her to meet most of the major figures in the Sadako story. As a second-generation A-bomb survivor, she regards this translation project as an important life work. She is presently in charge of international communication for Hiroshima Prefectural Medical Association.

How To Fold A Paper Crane

Learning to fold a crane by a set of diagrams is challenging and satisfying. If you get stuck, find a partner to help.

Key for the accompanying diagrams

● The shaded portions represent the colored side of the paper.

● Arrows indicate folding direction.

● Fine dotted lines indicate creases already made.

● Hyphenated lines indicate creases to be made.

Be sure to make all creases sharp.

1. Begin with a *square* piece of paper - ideally, one side colored and the other plain. Place the colored side face down on the table and fold the paper in half to form a rectangle. Think of this as folding to the 'East'.

1a. Unfold and fold in half to the 'North'.

1b. Unfold and fold paper diagonally (to the 'West') to form a triangle.

2. Unfold the paper and *turn it over* so that the colored side is up and fold to the 'South', to form a triangle.

Unfold the paper gently and push up from the white side of the paper. The center will *'pop'* up and two opposing quarters ,will bend inward along a diagonal valley.

3. Press on the centers of the two quarters that do *not* have the valleys and collapse the paper into a small square.

4. Taking the top flap of paper, fold the two upper sides so that they meet along the center guideline. (Note that point **a** is the 'open' end where all four corners of the paper come together.)

Take point **d** and fold down the top triangle along the line between points **b** and **c**.

Now it's time for the trickiest fold. Undo the folds you have just done in step 4. Lift the very top layer of paper at point **a**. Fold the paper up and back along lines **b-c** and make the figure lie flat in a long diamond by reversing the folds **a-b** and **b-c**. Think of this as opening a frog's mouth or the stretching of a wing to the sky.

Turn the paper over and repeat all of step 4 on the other side.

5. Now your paper looks like a diamond with two legs at the bottom. The next step is to taper the diamond at its legs by folding the sides of the top layer so that they meet at the center line. Turn over and repeat on other side to complete the tapering.

5a. Fold top right layer over the left. Turn over and repeat on other side.

6. Now you have a figure that looks like a fox with its pointy ears. Open the top layer of the fox's mouth from point **a** so that it touches the top of its ears.

Turn over and repeat on the other side.

7. Fold the top right layer over the left. Turn over and repeat on the other side.

8. You're almost done. Pull the crane is formed in its egg. Pull the narrow tips out a little bit from the base — to the left and right respectively. Press along the base to make them stay in place.

9. Form the head of the crane by taking one of the narrow tips and bending it down and pinching it so as to reverse the crease that makes the point.

10. Your finished crane! Open the body by gently pulling outward at the base of the two large flaps which form the wings.

**East north west south,
frog fox wing.
Old and young together make
an unexpected thing.**

Instructions copyright © 1990 by The Sadako Film Project, P.O. Box 67, Santa Cruz, CA 95063. This organization has produced a 30-minute video entitled *Sadako and the Thousand Paper Cranes*, narrated by Liv Ullmann, with music performed by George Winston, illustrated by Ed Young, and produced and directed by George Levenson. For more information call: 1 (800) 827-0949.